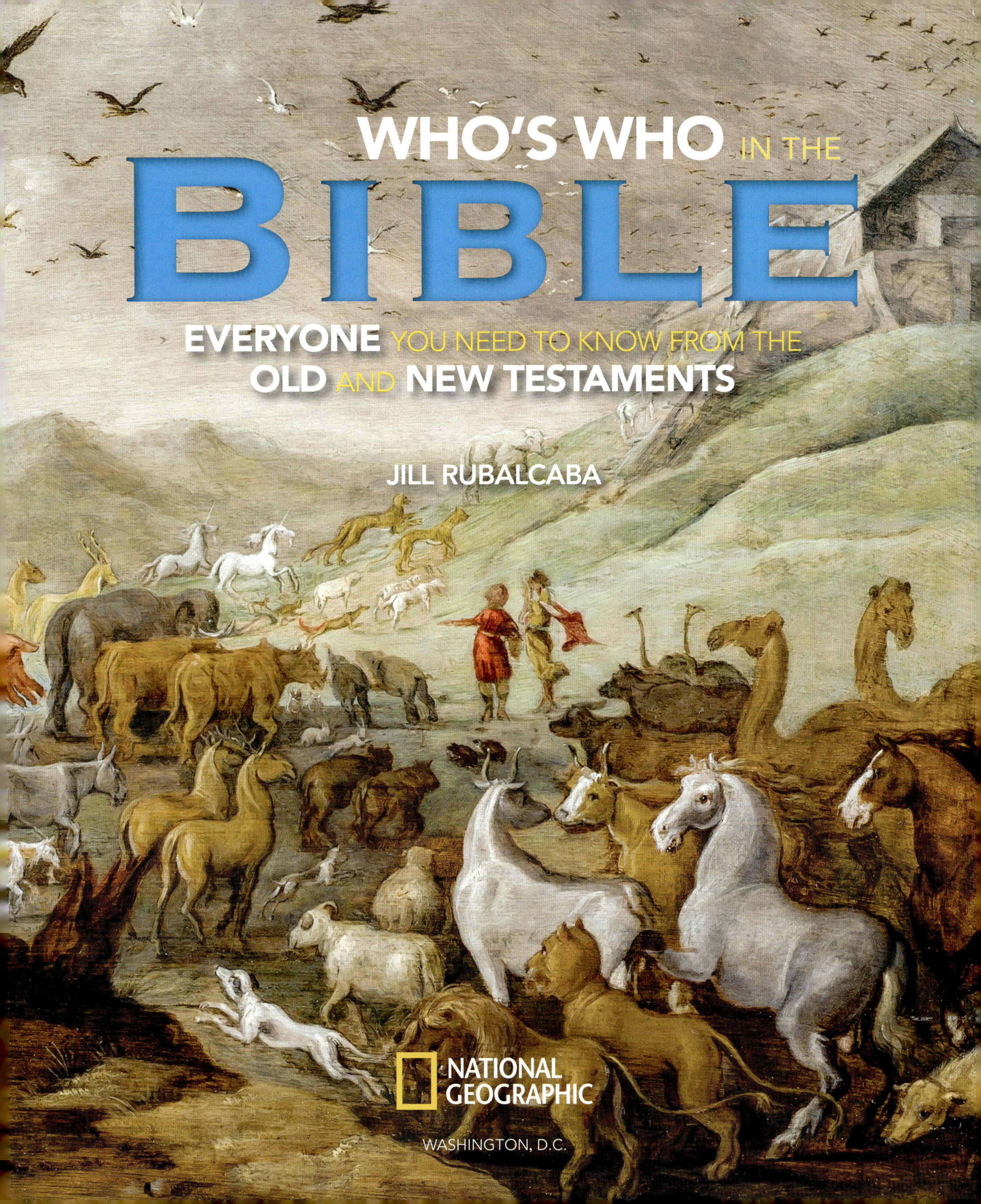

WHO'S WHO IN THE BIBLE

EVERYONE YOU NEED TO KNOW FROM THE OLD AND NEW TESTAMENTS

JILL RUBALCABA

NATIONAL GEOGRAPHIC

WASHINGTON, D.C.

JESUS, THE GOOD SHEPHERD

TABLE OF CONTENTS

Foreword

If there is one thing that has remained constant in our modern times, it is the Bible. No matter how much our daily world is transformed by new media and technologies, the people of the Bible are as vital and important today as they were thousands of years ago, when their stories were first written. Why is that, you ask? Because the people of the Bible, from the earliest stories of Genesis to the parables and teachings of Jesus, often faced questions that are very similar to what we see in our modern day: how to secure food and shelter and keep the family safe; how to live peacefully with other people in the community; how to resolve conflicts; and how to live happy and honest lives. The people in the Bible believed that this is what God wanted them to do because they believed that God is good and merciful—an incredible source of strength that could help them in times of trouble.

That is why this book is so timely, particularly for young readers. Now, more than ever, young people often face challenges of their own: at school, within their circle of friends, or on social media. We don't always know how to cope with such challenges, and sometimes we think that these problems are more than we can handle. At times like these, we may feel like Daniel, who was thrown in a den filled with lions waiting to devour him (as shown on the opposite page)!

Reading the stories of these biblical people and their incredible adventures not only illustrates their resourcefulness and their resilience, but also the idea that faith in a merciful God can help you overcome immense obstacles. If God split the waters of the sea so the Israelites could walk across, or poured down rain to stop an army of iron chariots dead in its tracks, then certainly God can be a source of strength and love in our own lives.

Who's Who in the Bible is a wonderful way to get to know the Bible, for both young readers who have never read scripture before and those well versed in biblical studies. The Bible is really composed of two separate parts: a Hebrew Bible (which Christians call the Old Testament) and a Christian Bible (the New Testament), which contains the four Gospels, apostolic letters, and the Book of Revelation. That is why the Bible is considered Judeo-Christian Scripture, because it really covers the aspirations of Jews and Christians in their search for God. Using wonderful illustrations and images, easy-to-read text, and intriguing sidebars, this book highlights both the differences and the many commonalities between the Hebrew and Christian Bibles. As such, it is a delightful publication for both browsing and reading, but can also be used for detailed reference.

Who's Who in the Bible is a book that no family should be without, regardless of background or faith orientation. It may serve as a perfect introduction to the Bible, which—even in the 21st century—remains an anchor of faith, ethics, and social justice.

Jean-Pierre Isbouts
Author of National Geographic's *The Biblical World* and *In the Footsteps of Jesus*

PEOPLE AND PLACES

Many people in the Bible lived within an area known today as the Fertile Crescent—crescent-shaped farmland between the Tigris and Euphrates Rivers. Other people, such as Alexander the Great and the Apostle Paul, ventured as far east as today's India and as far west as today's Italy. Archaeologists and historians have discovered much about the daily lives and customs of people of the Bible. The green boxes below indicate people from the Old Testament; the blue boxes, people from the New Testament.

IN THE BIBLICAL WORLD: 20TH CENTURY B.C.E. TO 1ST CENTURY C.E.

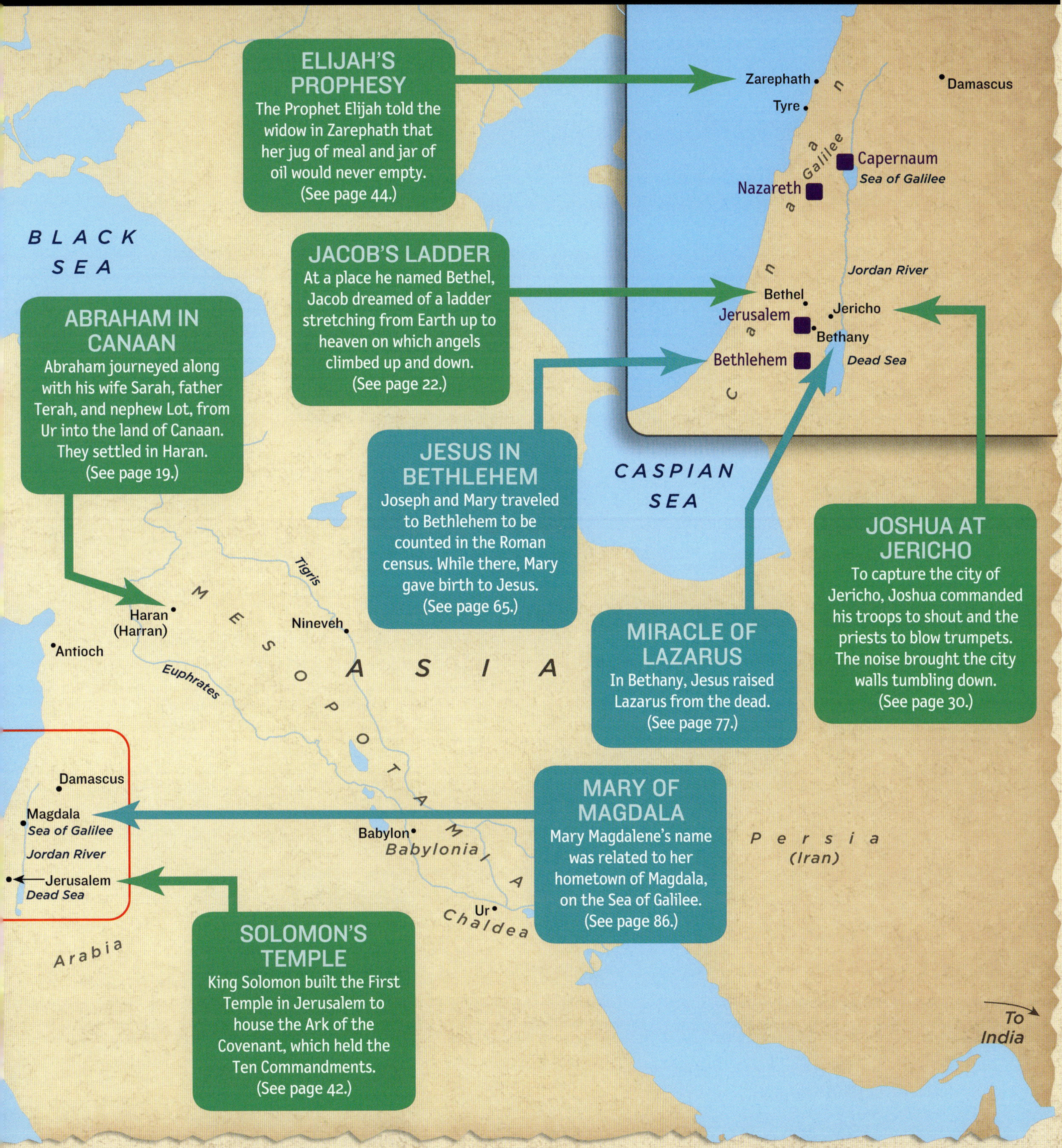

OLD TESTAMENT

INTRODUCTION

The Old Testament is the Christian name for what is known to Jews as the Hebrew Bible. It was taken from oral tradition and thought to have been written down by scribes between 1200 and 100 B.C.E. The stories they recorded were about events that had happened centuries before, some believe as early as the 18th century B.C.E.

Genesis, the first book of the Old Testament, starts with creation stories recording the very beginning of the universe. God had just created the first humans, Adam and Eve, and almost immediately they committed the very first sin. They disobeyed God by eating fruit he had forbidden. Humans continued to sin. After a while, God felt the need for a fresh start, and he sent a great flood to wipe out all living things. He spared the faithful Noah, his family, and a male and female of every animal.

With Abraham, the patriarch of a nomadic tribe, the story of God's chosen people begins. We follow Abraham and the tribe as they wander through Mesopotamia and then into Canaan. In Canaan God made a pact—called a covenant, or testament—with Abraham. This covenant lies at the heart of the Old Testament: follow God's law and Canaan, the "land of milk and honey," will belong to you and your descendants. Later, with Jacob, Abraham's grandson, God renewed this covenant. Jacob's 12 descendants led the 12 tribes of Israel, called the Israelites.

Moses is the hero of the second book, Exodus. He and his brother Aaron led the Israelites out of Egyptian slavery northward, toward Canaan. God revealed the Ten Commandments to Moses, and with them the covenant, or testament, was renewed yet again. If Moses and the people obeyed God's laws, he would lead them to the Promised Land.

The stories continue in the Books of Joshua and Judges, where it becomes clear that it will be hard to win possession of Canaan. The Philistines stood in the Israelites' way. David slayed the Philistine giant Goliath in an epic battle. In the Book of Samuel, the tribes of Israel finally united against their common enemy. The priest and prophet Samuel anointed Saul to be the first king of Israel. David, and then his descendants, ruled for the next four centuries with a brief interruption.

DAVID BRINGING THE ARK INTO JERUSALEM

The prophetic books in the Old Testament warned the people that God would punish them for their sins. But if they mended their ways, God would reward them. Three major prophets from these books—Isaiah, Jeremiah, and Ezekiel—each preached during different times, with different messages: Isaiah spoke out against Israel's corrupt rulers, predicting destruction, then restoration, of the land. Jeremiah blamed Israel's pagan worship for the fall of Jerusalem to the Babylonians. Ezekiel's visions reinforced their messages, but promised Israel's redemption.

Most books in the Old Testament are "wisdom books"—collections of histories, stories, poetry, and proverbs that taught about God and nature; they also offered guidance on how to live a good life. The 150 poetic songs in Psalms mention many of the people you will meet on the coming pages.

ADAM & EVE

ADAM

MEANING OF NAME "Man," "to be red"

BOOK Genesis **KNOWN FOR** First human man; naming all species; committing the original sin that barred humankind from paradise; first father

EVE

MEANING OF NAME The Hebrew is *hawwah*, which means "source of life"

BOOK Genesis **KNOWN FOR** First human female; committing the original sin that barred humankind from paradise; first mother

Adam is the first human to appear in the Bible. The second is Eve. We meet them in the first book of the Old Testament—Genesis. Genesis comes from the Greek word *gignesthai,* meaning "origin," and the Hebrew word *Bereishit,* meaning "in the beginning." Genesis introduces us to the first couple. Each of the personalities introduced in the following pages can trace his or her ancestry, or origins, back to Adam and Eve.

The biblical story of Adam and Eve begins in a lush botanical garden called Eden. In Eden, there was no disease or death, no violence or crime. Not even a dead blossom spoiled the perfection.

God created Adam from the rich earth and gave him life by blowing into Adam's nostrils. He placed Adam in the perfect garden with a few instructions. God told Adam he could eat the fruit from any tree in Eden—except from the Tree of Knowledge of Good and Evil. That was forbidden.

The first job God gave Adam was the task of naming all the birds and animals. One by one, God brought his creations to Adam for him to name. All the animals were in pairs, one male and one female. Adam realized he had no partner, and it made him feel lonely.

In Genesis 2:18, God said, "It is not good that the man should be alone; I will make him a helper as his partner." God put Adam into a deep sleep. While Adam slept, God removed one of his ribs and made Eve. When Adam awoke, he took one look at Eve and was delighted. When naming her he said, in Genesis 2:23, "This at last is bone of my bones, and flesh of my flesh; this one shall be called Woman, for out of Man this one was taken."

Adam and Eve lived carefree in paradise. They didn't even notice their nakedness—until a sly snake slithered into the picture. The snake convinced Eve that if she ate from the Tree of Knowledge she would become wise. Didn't she want to know things?

Eve did want to know things, and so she ate fruit from the tree.

Then Adam ate fruit from the tree.

Suddenly, they knew they were naked. They were embarrassed. Plucking broad fig leaves they tried to hide their bodies. And when they heard God walking in the garden, they hid.

But it is not easy to hide from God.

> ***"God formed man from the dust… and breathed into his nostrils the breath of life…."***
> ***—Genesis 2:7***

Punishment came swiftly. From then on, snakes would be forced to crawl in the dust. Women would suffer in childbirth, and men would toil in the fields. They all would know death. With God's curses hanging over their heads, Adam and Eve left Eden. God barred their return by placing ferocious guards at Eden's entrance and a rotating flaming sword in its center.

Eve is mentioned by name only once more in Genesis when she gave birth to sons Cain and Abel. Through references to Adam we know the original couple went on to have another son, Seth, when Adam was 130 years old. They had many more children over the next 800 years until, in Genesis 5, Adam died at the ripe old age of 930.

CREATION OF ADAM: One of the most copied religious images is Michelangelo's "The Creation of Adam," painted between 1508 and 1512 onto the ceiling of the Sistine Chapel in Vatican City. Michelangelo painted the creation scene while standing on scaffolding to reach the ceiling that rose 68 feet (21 m) into the air. Today it is where cardinals gather when it is time to choose a new pope.

CAIN & ABEL

CAIN
MEANING OF NAME "A possession," "a spear"
BOOK Genesis
KNOWN FOR The first farmer

ABEL
MEANING OF NAME "Breath," "emptiness," "vanity"
BOOK Genesis
KNOWN FOR The first shepherd

Not long after Adam and Eve were forced out of the Garden of Eden they had two children—Cain and Abel. Each followed a different way of life. Cain, who was born first, became a farmer, while Abel became a shepherd. After some time the brothers brought an offering to God, each from their own professions. Cain offered fruit, while Abel offered the best selections from his flock. God's preference for Abel's offering drove Cain mad with jealousy. In a fit of anger he killed his brother with a rock.

In Genesis 4:9, when God asked Cain, "Where's your brother Abel?" Cain answered, "I do not know; am I my brother's keeper?" But, of course, God already knew that Cain had murdered his brother. He confronted Cain, cursing him by turning the soil against him so that Cain could never farm again. Cain went on to live in the land of Nod—"the land of naught," or "no good." He married and had a son named Enoch.

FARMERS AND SHEPHERDS: Some experts think that the tensions between Cain and Abel in the Book of Genesis may represent the tensions between settled farmers and wandering shepherds in a region called the Levant, along the eastern Mediterranean Sea. Farmers settled down to tend to their plantings, such as olives, dates, and figs. Shepherds lived a nomadic existence, because herds in a dry climate need to keep moving to fresh fields for grazing.

CAIN, AT RIGHT, AND ABEL, AT LEFT, MAKE OFFERINGS TO GOD.

SETH

Seth was Adam and Eve's third son. He was born after the death of Abel when Adam was 130 years old. Eve believed that Seth was God's gift to replace her lost son. In Genesis 4:25, she said, "God has appointed for me another child instead of Abel..." Over the next 807 years, Seth fathered many sons and daughters. One of his descendants was Noah, the hero of the Great Flood story in Genesis. Seth died when he was 912 years old.

SETH **MEANING OF NAME** "Founder" **BOOK** Genesis **KNOWN FOR** Third son of Adam and Eve; ancestor to Noah

LEAH

Genesis 29:17 describes Leah, whose "eyes were lovely." She was Laban's eldest daughter and the first wife of Jacob (see page 22). Jacob was tricked into marrying Leah even though he was in love with Rachel. Together Jacob and Leah had six sons who founded six of the 12 tribes of Israel. They also had a daughter, Dinah.

LEAH **MEANING OF NAME** "Cow" or "gazelle" **BOOK** Genesis **KNOWN FOR** Mother of six tribes

BENJAMIN, STANDING AT CENTER

RACHEL

Laban's graceful and beautiful daughter, Rachel, fell in love with Jacob (see page 22) at first sight. And she was Jacob's one true love and beloved wife, even though Jacob had been tricked into first marrying Rachel's sister, Leah. After a long period of not being able to have children, Rachel finally had two sons—Joseph and then Benjamin. On a journey with Jacob from Bethel to Ephrath, Rachel went into labor and died giving birth to Benjamin.

RACHEL **MEANING OF NAME** "Ewe," a female sheep **BOOK** Genesis **KNOWN FOR** Great beauty; first person in the Bible to die in childbirth

RACHEL

BENJAMIN

In Genesis 49:27, while Jacob (see page 24) was on his deathbed he gave a final blessing to each of his 12 sons. To the youngest, Benjamin, he said: "Benjamin is a ravenous wolf, in the morning devouring the prey, and at evening dividing the spoil." Benjamin was the ancestor to one of the 12 tribes of Israel.

BENJAMIN **MEANING OF NAME** "Son of my right hand" **BOOK** Genesis **KNOWN FOR** Ancestor of the tribe of Benjamin

 NOAH, AT UPPER RIGHT, WATCHING THE ANIMALS BOARD THE ARK

NOAH

NOAH
MEANING OF NAME "Rest," "comfort"
BOOK Genesis
KNOWN FOR Second (after Adam) father of humankind; ark builder and survivor of the Great Flood

Without Noah, the list of personalities in the Bible would have been very short. God had become disgusted with the wicked ways of humans. Just ten generations after Adam and Eve, he was ready to blot out all living things and return Earth to its simpler state. And he would have—if it weren't for Noah. Noah had lived a good life, and God favored him for it.

Much of Genesis 6 describes building plans for an ark that God instructed Noah to build. It would house two of every animal as well as Noah and his wife; his three sons Shem, Ham, and Japheth; and their wives. The ark was huge—longer than a football field, half as wide, and almost four stories high. At that size, the ark could hold as many as 800 18-wheeler trucks.

"But Noah found favor in the sight of the Lord."
—Genesis 6:8

Just as soon as Noah had built the ark and loaded it according to God's commands, it began to rain—and rain and rain and rain—until the entire Earth was covered. Even the tallest mountains did not break the surface of the water. Months after the rain had stopped, the ark ran aground on the mountains of Ararat in present-day eastern Turkey. A year would pass before the earth dried up enough for all the creatures to leave the ark.

The first thing Noah did after setting foot on dry land was to build an altar. And the first thing God did was to send a rainbow through the clouds as a symbol of his promise to Noah that he would never flood Earth again. Genesis 9:14–15 explains that God told Noah, "When I bring clouds over the earth and the bow is seen in the clouds, I will remember my covenant that is between me and you and every living creature..."

Noah had always been a man of the soil, and even though he was more than 600 years old at this point, he decided to farm again. He planted a vineyard.

Noah died when he was 950 years old, 350 years after the flood.

THE SENIOR CITIZENS OF GENESIS 5: According to the Bible, people lived extraordinarily long lives before the flood. Genesis 5:27 says that Noah's grandfather Methuselah lived almost 1,000 years. But he would be considered a toddler by ancient records other than the Bible. One prism-shaped tablet made of clay, which was inscribed nearly 4,000 years ago in Sumer, listed the dates when eight Sumerian kings ruled. One king ruled for 43,200 years. Scientists debate the reason for such long lives before the flood. Did people at that time calculate years differently? Or did they say that kings ruled for long periods as a way to honor them? It is one more of the Bible's mysteries.

ABRAHAM

ABRAHAM
MEANING OF NAME Abram: "exalted father"; Abraham: "father of many"
BOOK Genesis
KNOWN FOR Unshakable faith; first to receive God's covenant; willingness to sacrifice his beloved son to God; ancestor to the 12 tribes

When we first meet Abraham he is named Abram, the eldest son of Terah. Terah and his family left the comfort of their home in Ur, in the area of present-day Iraq, and journeyed to Haran, in present-day Turkey. There, God ordered Abram to go to another "land that I will show you." Abram obeyed. When Abram, his wife Sarai, and his nephew Lot got as far as Canaan, God appeared again, telling Abram that this was the Promised Land where his descendants would give birth to a great nation.

Not long after they arrived in Canaan, a famine struck. In order to find food and fresh fields for their flocks, Abram, Sarai, and Lot were forced to keep moving—this time south to Egypt. Sarai's great beauty attracted the attention of the pharaoh, who brought her into his palace. When the pharaoh discovered that Sarai was married, he released her and sent her and her family back to Canaan, allowing them to keep the wealth they had built up while in Egypt.

Abram and Lot owned a large number of grazing animals. Their herdsmen quarreled over where their animals could eat. To settle the dispute, Abram gave Lot first pick of grazing land. Lot chose the green and fertile plain of Sodom and Gomorrah. Not long after, Lot and his family were taken prisoner by local rulers. Abram assembled warriors and rode to the rescue, freeing his nephew and the others who had been captured.

Abram and Sarai were still childless when God repeated his promise to bless them with offspring as numerous as stars in the sky. Sarai, convinced that she and Abram would never have children of their own, talked Abram into having a child with their Egyptian slave, Hagar. Sarai's plan worked, and Hagar bore Abram a son, Ishmael.

God appeared to Abram yet again, repeating his promise that Abram and Sarai would have many children. He changed Abram's name to Abraham, which means "father of many," and from then on Sarai was to be called Sarah.

As God had promised, despite her advanced age, Sarah gave birth to a boy, Isaac. Following Isaac's birth, the conflicts between Sarah and Hagar became so intense Abraham was forced to send Hagar and Ishmael away.

As painful as it was to turn away his son Ishmael, it did not compare to the anguish he would soon suffer. God commanded Abraham to sacrifice his beloved son Isaac. Steadfast in his faith, Abraham did not hesitate in preparing to sacrifice Isaac. He bound Isaac's hands and laid him on a huge stone as an altar. At the last moment, when Abraham's knife was poised to kill Isaac, an angel appeared and stopped him, "Do not lay your hand on the boy…for now I know that you fear God." Abraham had proved that his faith was unshakable.

It was through Abraham and Sarah's son Isaac, and Isaac's son Jacob, and Jacob's 12 sons that the 12 tribes of Israel were founded. God's promise of founding a great nation was fulfilled.

ABRAHAM'S BIRTHPLACE: Abraham's possible birthplace, the Mesopotamian city of Ur, in present-day Iraq, was once a bustling port city on the Persian Gulf. Merchants imported luxury goods from as far away as India. An 80-foot (24-m)-tall tower called a ziggurat stood at the city's center. The highly civilized city of learning and culture was gradually abandoned because of land overuse and because a changing climate caused the waters to recede.

SARAH

SARAH
MEANING OF NAME "Princess"
BOOK Genesis
KNOWN FOR Wife of Abraham; mother of Isaac

Like many people in the Bible, when we initially meet Sarah in Genesis 11, she has a different name—Sarai, which God later changes to Sarah. The first thing we learn about Sarah is that she is married to Abraham and she cannot have children.

Apparently, Sarah was extraordinarily beautiful. When they were forced to move to Egypt because of a famine, Abraham worried that the Egyptians would kill him in order to take Sarah for themselves. Sarah agreed to pretend to be Abraham's sister instead of his wife. The pharaoh did fancy Sarah and took her into his house, rewarding her "brother" with livestock and slaves. When the pharaoh discovered the truth about Sarah, he returned her to Abraham.

This was not the only time Sarah had to pretend she was Abraham's sister. In Genesis 20, on a journey to Gerar, Abraham told King Abimelech that Sarah was his sister because he feared the king would kill him and take Sarah. God appeared to the king in a dream and revealed the truth, and the king apologized to Abraham. He gave Abraham livestock, slaves, and silver and then returned Sarah.

Toward the end of her life God blessed Sarah with a son, Isaac. Sarah died at the age of 127 years. Heartbroken, Abraham purchased the Cave of Machpelah and buried her facing Hebron, in the land of Canaan. In Genesis 13, he had settled his family and built an altar to God in Hebron. Present-day Hebron is on Palestine's West Bank, just south of Jerusalem.

"...the Lord did for Sarah as he had promised. Sarah conceived and bore Abraham a son in his old age...."
—Genesis 21:1–2

UNDERGROUND CAVE: The Cave of Machpelah is also known as the Cave of the Patriarchs. It is a series of underground caves beneath today's city of Hebron. Genesis 23 tells how Abraham purchased the cave from the Hittites as a burial place for his beloved Sarah. Abraham, Isaac, Jacob, Rebekah, and Leah were also buried there. Two thousand years ago, King Herod built a massive structure over the graves to provide a place for people to gather and pray. They still do to this day.

SARAH, AT LEFT, AND THREE TRAVELERS

ISAAC

ISAAC
MEANING OF NAME "Laughter"
BOOK Genesis
KNOWN FOR The longest living of the three patriarchs Abraham, Isaac, and Jacob

In Genesis 17, Abraham and his wife Sarah were very old when God said to Abraham, "I will bless [Sarah] and I will give you a son by her...she shall give rise to nations." The couple were so old that Abraham "fell on his face and laughed." But God said, "No, Sarah shall bear you a son, and you shall name him Isaac." When Isaac was born, Abraham was 100 years old and Sarah was 90. Later, in Genesis 22, it would be Isaac who Abraham would nearly sacrifice to honor God's request. Only at the last minute would an angel stop him.

In the years after that test, Sarah died. Abraham was very old now and he wanted to find a wife for Isaac—preferably someone from his own tribe. In Genesis 24, Abraham sent a trusted servant to Haran to find Isaac a wife with God's guidance. The servant returned with Rebekah, who had agreed to marry Isaac.

Isaac was walking in the fields when he noticed several camels approaching. Rebekah, who had been riding one of the camels, slipped to the ground. The servant told Isaac how he had found Rebekah, while she stood by listening, modestly covered with a veil. Isaac then took Rebekah to the tent that had been his mother's. There Rebekah became Isaac's wife.

After Isaac's father died, Isaac and Rebekah found out they were expecting twins. God told them that the twins—Esau and Jacob—would establish two nations.

Esau, who was born first, was Isaac's favorite, and Jacob was Rebekah's. When Isaac was old and blind, Rebekah and Jacob tricked him into giving Esau's inheritance as the oldest son to Jacob.

Finally, Isaac breathed his last breath at 180 years of age; his sons Esau and Jacob buried him.

ISAAC, AT RIGHT, BLESSES JACOB.

STONE SHRINE: In the old part of Jerusalem, a Muslim shrine called the Dome of the Rock was built over the place where tradition says that Abraham placed his son Isaac, preparing to sacrifice him to God.

JACOB & ESAU

JACOB & ESAU

MEANING OF NAME Jacob: "heel," "grasper"; Esau: "hairy"

BOOK Genesis

KNOWN FOR Fathers of two nations: Jacob was renamed Israel in Genesis 32:28 and became the ancestor of the 12 tribes; Esau fathered the Edomites, according to Genesis 36:1–9

Genesis 25–27 tells the story of Isaac and Rebekah's twin sons. The hairy, redheaded Esau came first. He was followed by Jacob, who was grasping Esau's heel. Jacob's name comes from the Hebrew word *ya'agov*, whose root means "heel." The boys grew up to pursue different things and to appeal to different parents. Esau loved the outdoors and spent his days hunting, so Isaac, also a hunter, favored him. Jacob was much quieter and enjoyed staying at home, so Rebekah the homemaker felt closer to him.

Jacob wanted his older brother's inheritance, and with the help of Rebekah he tricked Isaac to get it. Dressing up as the hairy Esau and preparing a special feast, he asked Isaac, now old and blind, for his blessing. Touching the hairy costume and eating the food, Isaac thought this was Esau and readily gave the blessing. Esau was furious and wanted to kill Jacob, so Jacob fled north to live with his uncle Laban. During his journey, Jacob dreamed of a ladder stretching up into heaven with angels climbing up and down. Realizing this place must be important to God he named it Bethel, which means "House of God."

"Esau said to his father, 'Have you only one blessing, father? Bless me, me also, father!'"
—Genesis 27:38

Once Jacob arrived at his destination of Paddan Aram, in present-day Turkey, he met Laban's daughter Rachel and fell in love. Jacob worked for Laban for seven years to earn her hand in marriage, but on the wedding day he was tricked by Laban, who switched the older sister, Leah, for Rachel. Jacob married Leah, but he worked another seven years for Rachel's hand, and six more for cattle.

RECONCILIATION OF ESAU, AT LEFT, AND JACOB

Jacob had now become wealthy, which made his father-in-law's family jealous. In Genesis 31, God told Jacob it was time to go home. He returned to his homeland of Canaan with Leah and Rachel. Once during the journey, Jacob wrestled all night with a stranger who likely was God in the form of an angel. By the time Jacob arrived home, time had healed the wounds between Jacob and Esau, and they met with a warm embrace. In Genesis 32, God gave Jacob a new name—Israel, which means "he who prevails with God." Jacob had 12 sons, and his descendants became the leaders of the 12 tribes of Israel.

RUBENS' PAINTING: The Flemish painter Peter Paul Rubens was so popular he hired assistants to keep up with the demand for his work. Rubens himself created this oil sketch (above) for the painting "The Reconciliation of Jacob and Esau." It depicts the scene when Jacob came home years after he tricked his brother Esau, and he was immediately forgiven. Rubens' assistants made the final painting sometime around 1625.

JOSEPH

JOSEPH
MEANING OF NAME "Taken away," "God adds"
BOOK Genesis
KNOWN FOR Favored son of Jacob; sold into slavery by his brothers; second most powerful man in Egypt

Jacob fathered 12 sons. Joseph, the second youngest, was Jacob's favorite. Joseph and his brothers were shepherds for Jacob's flocks. Genesis 37 tells how Jacob made Joseph a special robe, a luxury for a shepherd. It had long sleeves, which were difficult to produce on the looms of that period. In addition, Jacob had dreams that told him Joseph would be a leader to the others. His brothers became so jealous that they plotted to kill Joseph. Only his brother Reuben showed mercy. He convinced the others to throw Joseph into a pit and not shed Joseph's blood. Secretly, Reuben planned on rescuing Joseph after the others had gone. However, once Reuben left, Joseph's brothers pulled him out of the pit and sold him as a slave to traders whose caravan happened to be passing by on the way to Egypt.

In Egypt, the traders sold Joseph to Potiphar, the pharaoh's captain of the guard. But Potiphar's wife and Joseph had a falling out, which ended with Joseph being sent to prison.

While in prison Joseph interpreted the dreams of the pharaoh's cupbearer and baker. When the pharaoh learned of Joseph's talent he sent for Joseph to interpret his own dream. Joseph told the pharaoh that the seven fat cows in his dream meant seven years of abundant crops, and the seven scrawny cows meant seven years of famine. The pharaoh was so pleased with Joseph that he made him his second-in-command, overseeing all of Egypt.

Jacob believed that Joseph was dead and mourned him. Later, in Genesis 42–46, the brothers went to Egypt to purchase grain and did not recognize Joseph. When he revealed himself, they were shocked that he was alive and so powerful. He treated them well and sent gifts home to an overjoyed Jacob, who came to live near Joseph.

JOSEPH, IN A PINK ROBE, IS SOLD INTO SLAVERY.

JOSEPH'S ROBE: According to Genesis, when Joseph was 17 his father gave him a robe. But what kind of robe? What style and color? There are many descriptions of it, depending on the translation of the Hebrew or Greek words for Jacob's robe: "a long robe with sleeves," "a coat of many colors," "a fine woolen cloak," "a silk robe," "a coat reaching to his feet," "embroidered," "striped," or even "with pictures." Whatever the robe looked like, it made his brothers so jealous they plotted his death.

THE TWELVE TRIBES OF ISRAEL

According to the Bible, Jacob's descendants founded the 12 tribes of Israel. In Genesis 49, while Jacob lay on his deathbed, he gave each of his 12 sons a blessing, predicting their futures as leaders of nations. Many scholars count the 12 brothers as the heads of the 12 tribes of Israel. Others count the leaders of Israel's 12 tribal territories (see map, opposite). Later, in the Book of Joshua, the Israelite leader Joshua gives Jacob's sons different territories in Canaan, the Promised Land. Jacob's son Levi, a priest, did not take a territory, but accepted cities all over the Promised Land. Joseph, Jacob's favored son, received two territories, but gave them away—one to each of his two sons, Ephraim and Manasseh. Below is the story of the leaders and where they settled.

GENESIS 29

BORN: Genesis 29:32 | Genesis 29:33 | Genesis 29:34 | Genesis 29:35 | Genesis 30:4–6 | Genesis 30:7–8 | Genesis 30:10–11

REUBEN ("BEHOLD THE SON")

Jacob's son with Leah

Reuben was the only brother to try to save Joseph when the other jealous brothers plotted to kill him. The tribe of Reuben settled east of the Jordan River.

SIMEON ("GOD HAS HEARD")

Jacob's son with Leah

Simeon and his brothers brought Benjamin to see Joseph, who was safe in Egypt. Joseph allowed the others to return home but put Simeon in jail as insurance that the others would return. The tribe of Simeon settled in the southernmost part of the Israelites' territory.

LEVI ("JOINED")

Jacob's son with Leah

Levi, along with Simeon, killed Shechem, prince of the city of Shechem, and all the men in his city to avenge the honor of their sister Dinah. The priestly tribe of Levi occupied 48 cities spread throughout the 12 territories.

JUDAH ("PRAISE")

Jacob's son with Leah

After Solomon's death in I Kings, Israel split into two kingdoms, the southern kingdom was known as the kingdom of Judah, which included Jerusalem and Bethlehem. It was an independent kingdom until the Babylonians conquered it in II Kings. Historians determined that this was three centuries later, around 2600 B.C.E.

DAN ("JUDGE")

Jacob's son with Bilhah, Rachel's servant

In Genesis 49:17, Jacob's deathbed blessing for Dan is: "Dan shall be a snake by the roadside, a viper along the path." The tribe of Dan settled above the tribe of Judah.

NAPHTALI ("WRESTLING")

Jacob's son with Bilhah, Rachel's servant

The Song of Deborah in Judges 5 describes the brave soldiers from the Naphtali tribe. The tribe of Naphtali settled in the northern part of Canaan.

GAD ("TROOP," "INVADER," "GOOD FORTUNE")

Jacob's son with Zilpah, Leah's servant

Jacob's deathbed blessing predicted that Gad would never be conquered. The tribe of Gad settled on the eastern bank of the Jordan River, north of the Dead Sea.

THE NEGEV (DESERT), IN ISRAEL

JOSEPH, AT RIGHT, INTERPRETS PHARAOH'S DREAM.

Asher ("Happy")

Jacob's son with Zilpah, Leah's servant

Jacob blessed Asher with food fit for royalty. The tribe of Asher settled along the Mediterranean coast just north of Mount Carmel.

Zebulun ("Dwelling")

Jacob's son with Leah

Jacob's last words to his son Zebulun in Genesis 49:13 were: "Zebulun shall settle at the shore of the sea; he shall be a haven for ships..." The tribe of Zebulun settled in central Galilee in the northern part of Canaan.

Joseph ("Increase")

Jacob's son with Rachel

His brothers sold him into slavery in Egypt, but he became a great man there. Joseph gave the land he inherited in Canaan to his two sons Manasseh and Ephraim. Later, in the Book of Exodus, when Moses and the Israelites escaped, Moses carried Joseph's bones from Egypt to be buried in Joseph's home of Shechem, in Canaan.

GENESIS 49

Genesis 30:12–13 Genesis 30:17–18 Genesis 30:19–20 Genesis 30:22–24 Genesis 35:16–18 BLESSED: Genesis 48:9–22 BLESSED: Genesis 49:1–29

Issachar ("Man of Hire")

Jacob's son with Leah

Joshua 17:10 tells how the tribe of Issachar settled between the tribes of Ephraim, Manasseh, and Asher, just south of the Sea of Galilee and east of the Jordan River.

Benjamin ("Son of My Right Hand")

Jacob's son with Rachel

The first king of the Jews, Saul, was from Benjamin's tribe. The tribe of Benjamin's territory included the cities of Jericho and Jerusalem in central Canaan.

Manasseh ("Forgetting")

Joseph's son, Jacob's grandson

As Jacob neared death in Genesis 48, he accepted Joseph's sons Manasseh and Ephraim as his own sons. Joseph gave his land to them: The tribe of Manasseh was allotted the most land, reaching from the Mediterranean Sea inland to the Jordan River.

Ephraim ("Double Fruitfulness")

Joseph's son, Jacob's grandson

Although Ephraim was younger than Manasseh, Genesis 48:19 explains that he received the greater blessing from Jacob, which was usually the first son's birthright. "His offspring shall become a multitude of nations," Jacob said. The tribe of Ephraim settled in the central region, on either side of the Jordan River.

Blessing of the Sons

On his deathbed in Genesis 49, Jacob blessed each of his 12 sons "with a suitable blessing."

Reuben: "you are my firstborn"; Simeon and Levi: "weapons of violence are their swords"; Judah: "your brothers shall praise you"; Zebulun: "shall settle at the shore of the sea"; Issachar: "is a strong donkey"; Dan: "shall judge his people"; Gad: "shall be raided by raiders"; Asher: his "food shall be rich"; Naphtali: "a doe let loose"; Joseph: "a fruitful bough"; Benjamin: "a ravenous wolf."

 MOSES WITH THE TEN COMMANDMENTS

Moses

MOSES

MEANING OF NAME In Egyptian, "begotten," "born"; in Hebrew, Mosheh sounded like *mashah*, which means "drawn out"

BOOK Exodus, Leviticus, Numbers, Deuteronomy

KNOWN FOR Prophet; Egyptian prince; leading the Jews out of Egypt; lawgiver; performing miracles; biblical author

The fortunes of the Israelites took a dramatic turn between the end of the Book of Genesis, where they were prospering in Egypt, and the beginning of the Book of Exodus, where they were now suffering in slavery. The Egyptian pharaoh was threatened by the increasing number of Israelites and ordered all Israelite baby boys to be thrown into the Nile. Moses escaped this fate when he was rescued by the pharaoh's daughter, brought into the royal household, and raised to adulthood under her protection.

> **"Never since has there arisen a prophet in Israel like Moses, whom the Lord knew face to face."**
> ***—Deuteronomy 34:10***

As a young man in Exodus 2, Moses was forced to flee Egypt after murdering an Egyptian who was beating an Israelite. He ended up in Midian, on today's Arabian Peninsula, among tent-dwelling nomads. There, he met and married Zipporah, daughter of the local priest. One day while Moses was tending his father-in-law's flock, God called to him from a burning bush. In Exodus 3:8, God gives Moses the mission to lead the Israelites out of Egypt to "a land flowing with milk and honey..."

Moses, along with Zipporah, their sons, and his brother Aaron, traveled by donkey to Egypt to free the Israelites. But when they delivered God's message in Exodus 5:1, to "let my people go," the pharaoh only made life more difficult for the enslaved Israelites. The pharaoh continued to refuse Moses and Aaron's request, even after they performed miracles as the pharaoh demanded, such as Aaron turning his staff into a snake. At last, God sent ten plagues. After the tenth plague, which killed all the firstborn Egyptians and creatures in Egypt, the pharaoh could bear no more and relented. The Israelites were allowed to leave. According to Exodus 12:39, the Israelites quickly packed their things and fled, not even waiting for their bread dough to rise.

Moses led the Egyptians into the wilderness. When they reached the Red Sea, they discovered that the pharaoh had a change of heart and was pursuing them. God told Moses to lift his staff and part the sea, exposing a pathway for escape. The Egyptian horses and chariots bore down on them, but Moses turned and raised his hand, and God sent the waters crashing back upon the army, drowning the soldiers.

On the Israelites' trek through the desert they complained of hunger and thirst, but God provided. Each morning they found a food called manna covering the ground. At last they arrived at Mount Sinai, which some believe may be on the present-day Sinai Peninsula. Here, in Exodus 20, Moses received the Ten Commandments from God. While Moses was on Mount Sinai, the Israelites below, led by Aaron, were already breaking the first two commandments—to honor only God and never to pray to an idol. They were worshipping a golden calf. As punishment, God ordered the Israelites to wander in the wilderness for 40 years, until that entire generation was gone. Only their descendants would be allowed into the Promised Land. Not even Moses would see it.

At the end of his life, Moses climbed Mount Nebo, in present-day Jordan, and there God let him look out over the land of Canaan his descendants would inherit. Deuteronomy 34:7–8 tells us, "Moses was a hundred and twenty years old when he died; his sight was unimpaired and his vigor had not abated. The Israelites wept for Moses in the plains of Moab thirty days; then the period of mourning for Moses was ended."

SETTLERS IN CANAAN: Here the Israelites became farmers, growing wheat, barley, and flax and using wooden plows pulled by oxen. Archaeologists have discovered a boom in population during the 12th century B.C.E. along the western bank of the Jordan River between Hebron and Shechem, supporting the Bible's description of settlers in Canaan.

Moses' Inner Circle

The following people played parts in Moses' life and journeys in the Old Testament.

Amram

Amram was Moses' father, and from the tribe of Levi.

AMRAM **MEANING OF NAME** "An exalted people," "kindred of the high" **BOOK** Exodus, Numbers **KNOWN FOR** Moses' father

Jochebed

To save her son from the pharaoh's order to kill Jewish baby boys, Jochebed coated a basket with tar, placed baby Moses in the basket, and hid it among the reeds.

JOCHEBED **MEANING OF NAME** "Whose glory is God" **BOOK** Exodus, Numbers **KNOWN FOR** Moses' mother; hid Moses for three months; put Moses in a basket and placed it on the bank of the Nile

ELEAZAR, KNEELING, BEING BLESSED AS A HIGH PRIEST

MIRIAM

Miriam

Prophet, poet, and musician, Moses' older sister Miriam was leader of the Israelite women as they followed Moses toward the Promised Land. Miriam's jealousy of Moses provoked God into striking her with leprosy.

MIRIAM **MEANING OF NAME** "Bitterness" **BOOK** Exodus **KNOWN FOR** Moses' older sister; boldly telling the pharaoh's daughter she would find a wet nurse (her mother) for Moses; prophetess; led the women of Israel in song after the parting of the Red Sea

Aaron

Aaron supported his younger brother Moses whenever Moses lost confidence and felt self-doubt.

AARON **MEANING OF NAME** "Lofty," "mountain of strength" **BOOK** Exodus, Chronicles, Deuteronomy, Psalms, Leviticus, Numbers **KNOWN FOR** Moses' older brother; Moses' spokesperson; one of the most important high priests in the Bible; accompanied Moses during audiences with the pharaoh; made the golden calf while Moses was on Mount Sinai

Jethro

Jethro, Moses' father-in-law, advised Moses not to take on the task of sole judge, but rather to teach others the law and select trustworthy judges to decide the less important cases.

JETHRO **MEANING OF NAME** "Excellence" **BOOK** Exodus, Numbers **KNOWN FOR** Moses' father-in-law; priest of Midian; guided the Israelites out of Sinai and into the Promised Land

ZIPPORAH

One of Jethro's seven daughters, Zipporah was Moses' wife and the mother of their two children, Gershom and Eliezer.

ZIPPORAH **MEANING OF NAME** "Beauty" **BOOK** Exodus **KNOWN FOR** Moses' wife; mother of Gershom and Eliezer

GERSHOM

In Exodus 2:22, Moses said he named his oldest son Gershom because "I have been an alien residing in a foreign land."

GERSHOM **MEANING OF NAME** "A stranger or alien," "exile" **BOOK** Exodus **KNOWN FOR** Moses' oldest son

ELEAZAR

Eleazar was responsible for carrying many sacred objects used in the Tabernacle—the tent of worship—brought by the Israelites while they wandered through the desert during the Exodus.

ELEAZAR **MEANING OF NAME** "God has helped" **BOOK** Exodus, Leviticus, Numbers, Joshua, Samuel **KNOWN FOR** Moses' nephew; high priest; helped Moses take a count of the male Israelites who were fit to be soldiers; allotted land taken in conquest to the Israelites

ELISHEBA

The Bible says little about Aaron's wife other than that she was the daughter of Amminadab and the sister of Nahshon.

ELISHEBA **MEANING OF NAME** "God is her oath," "God will restore" **BOOK** Exodus **KNOWN FOR** Moses' sister-in-law; wife of Aaron; mother of Nadab, Abihu, Eleazar, and Ithamar

"Moses was instructed in all the wisdom of the Egyptians and was powerful in his words and deeds."
—Acts 7:22

MOSES WITH JOSHUA, AT LEFT

JOSHUA

Next to Aaron, Joshua was Moses' most important assistant. He became the leader of the Israelites after Moses' death. (See page 30.)

JOSHUA **MEANING OF NAME** "God is salvation" **BOOK** Exodus, Chronicles, Numbers, Joshua **KNOWN FOR** Chosen by Moses to lead the Israelites against Amalek; sent by Moses to explore Canaan

CALEB

Moses sent one scout from each of the tribes of Israel to go ahead to the Promised Land and return with a report. Only Caleb and Joshua gave positive impressions. The other 10 claimed that their mission was impossible.

CALEB **MEANING OF NAME** "A dog" **BOOK** Chronicles, Numbers, Joshua **KNOWN FOR** Scout from the tribe of Judah

JOSHUA

JOSHUA
MEANING OF NAME "God saves"
BOOK Joshua, Exodus, Numbers, Deuteronomy
KNOWN FOR Leading the Israelites after Moses; turning Jericho's walls into rubble

After Moses died, God chose Joshua to lead the Israelites across the Jordan River and into Canaan, the Promised Land. Under Moses, Joshua had been the leader of a small army that defended the Israelites against enemies during their journey. Now he faced a new challenge. Before the Israelites could enter Canaan, Joshua and his army had to take military possession of the land. First they had to capture the heavily walled city of Jericho, which stood in the way. Unlike the great armies of Egypt, Canaan, Philistine, and Assyria, Joshua's army did not have the modern weapons of the day—no battering rams, chariots, or complex bows for their arrows. What the Israelites did have was the sacred Ark of the Covenant that held God's Ten Commandments—and a plan from God.

The Book of Joshua tells how the army followed God's plan. For six days Joshua and his troops marched around the impenetrable city wall. Seven priests, blowing seven rams' horns, marched in front of the Ark, leading all of Joshua's warriors. On the seventh day, says Joshua 6:16–20, they circled the wall seven times and then let out one long blast from the horns. That was the signal for the Israelites to shout at the top of their lungs. It worked. The walls came tumbling down. Joshua and his army charged into the heart of the city and captured Jericho.

One by one, the Canaanite kingdoms fell to Joshua's army. When all Canaan was won, the land was divided among the 12 tribes of Israel, as God had instructed. His mission accomplished, Joshua died at 110 years old and was buried in the hill country of Ephraim, the central territory among the 12 tribes.

JERICHO: Between 1907 and 2014, four excavations were conducted at the site of the fortified city of Jericho, located on Palestine's West Bank, near the Jordan River. Archaeologists have uncovered city walls that have been built, destroyed, and rebuilt many times over thousands of years.

JOSHUA ON HORSE AT JERICHO

BARAK, DELILAH, RUTH, JESSE

RUTH AND BOAZ

BARAK

In the Book of Judges, Barak, an Israelite judge and military commander for the judge and military leader Deborah (see page 34), led a force of 10,000 men from the tribes of Zebulun and Naphtali against the superior Canaanite army led by General Sisera. According to Judges 4:15 and 5:21, God unleashed a rainstorm, which threw Sisera's army into a panic; then the swollen waters of the Kishon River swept the Canaanites away. For the next 40 years, Israel enjoyed peace.

BARAK **MEANING OF NAME** "Lightning" **BOOK** Judges **KNOWN FOR** Defeating the Canaanite army as the general of the judge Deborah; ruler and judge

DELILAH

Delilah came from the valley of Sorek, in Philistia, the country of the Philistines, which shared a border with Israel. In Judges 16, the Israelite judge Samson, who had superhuman strength, fell in love with her. Delilah betrayed Samson by revealing the secret of his strength to his enemies, the Philistines, for a fortune in silver.

DELILAH **MEANING OF NAME** "Languishing" **BOOK** Judges **KNOWN FOR** Tricking Samson into revealing the source of his power and then selling the information to the Philistines

RUTH

After both their husbands died in the country of Moab, Ruth traveled with her mother-in-law, Naomi, to Bethlehem. There, Ruth met and married Boaz. They had a son, Obed, who became the grandfather of King David. Ruth's story, in the Book of Ruth, is read each year by rabbis at her tomb in Hebron.

RUTH **MEANING OF NAME** "Beloved" **BOOK** Ruth, Matthew **KNOWN FOR** Heroine in the Book of Ruth; great-grandmother of King David; one of five women mentioned in the lineage of Jesus, who descended from David

JESSE

Jesse, the grandson of Ruth and son of Obed, was a wealthy sheep farmer in Bethlehem. The youngest of Jesse's eight sons, David, became king of the Israelites.

JESSE **MEANING OF NAME** "God exists," "God's gift" **BOOK** Isaiah, Ruth, I Samuel **KNOWN FOR** King David's father; mentioned in the lineage of Jesus

DELILAH AND THE PHILISTINES

Pharaohs of Ancient Egypt

Throughout the Bible—especially in the Old Testament—there are many verses that mention the land of Egypt and its kings, who were called pharaohs. Sometimes no specific ruler is named—there is just a mention of "the pharaoh." Among the most vivid stories are those surrounding Moses and "the pharaoh." And yet no specific ruler is named. Who was this man who the Bible says enslaved the Israelites and whose "heart hardened" as he endured plague after plague sent from God, until he had no choice but to let the Israelites go? Archaeologists have sometimes compared pharaohs referenced in the Bible with real pharaohs they have studied. Read the stories of some of the Bible's pharaohs below.

Genesis 12:10–20

Pharaoh and Sarah

An unnamed pharaoh fell under the spell of Sarah's great beauty. Thinking she was Abraham's sister, he took Sarah into his palace and befriended Abraham. When the pharaoh discovered that God was punishing him with plagues because Sarah was actually Abraham's wife, he sent both Abraham and Sarah away.

Genesis 41

Pharaoh and Joseph

Joseph interpreted an unnamed pharaoh's dream. The pharaoh was so pleased that he gave Joseph an important position in charge of all of Egypt's food supply. By storing grain during seven years of plenty, Joseph saved the Egyptians from starvation during seven years of famine.

Exodus 1:8

Seti I

This passage says that a "new king" came to power and proceeded to rule during the time the Israelites were enslaved in Egypt. Some archaeologists think this unnamed pharaoh could have been Seti I, who they have determined ruled from 1291 to 1279 B.C.E.

Exodus 6:11

Ramses II

God told Moses, "Go and tell Pharaoh king of Egypt to let the Israelites go out of his land." Some experts think this pharaoh may have been Ramses II, who followed Seti I. They have determined that Ramses II ruled from 1279 to 1212 B.C.E. If Ramses II did follow Seti I, he would have been the pharaoh who endured the ten plagues sent by God before letting the Israelites go.

I Kings 3

Pharaoh and Solomon

Solomon married the daughter of an unnamed pharaoh to create an alliance between Israel and Egypt.

I Kings 14:25–26; II Chronicles 12:2–9

Shishak

Pharaoh Shishak attacked Jerusalem, in Judah, with 1,200 chariots and 60,000 cavalry. Solomon's son Rehoboam was king of Judah at the time. Shishak raided the temple and Rehoboam's palace, taking everything of value, including the guards' shields made of gold. Experts have determined that Shishak ruled from 945 to 924 B.C.E.

THE ISRAELITES ESCAPE FROM EGYPT THROUGH THE RED SEA.

THE PYRAMIDS OF GIZA, IN EGYPT

MOSES

TIRHAKA (TAHARQA)

These passages mention Tirhakah, calling him the king of Ethiopia. In Egyptian historical documents this is Pharaoh Taharqa, who ruled from 690 to 664 B.C.E. Historians have determined that Taharqa battled with Sennacherib of Assyria at the time Hezekiah was the king of Judah, a conflict also mentioned in the Bible.

NECO (NECHO II)

Pharaoh Neco's archers killed King Josiah of Judah in the plain of Megiddo. Pharaoh Neco then placed his own brother on Judah's throne. Archaeologists have determined that a pharaoh named Necho II ruled from 610 to 595 B.C.E. with a history that echoes this biblical account.

HOPHRA

God directed the Prophet Jeremiah to bury large stones in front of Pharaoh Hophra's palace so that King Nebuchadnezzar of Babylon could sit on top of the stones. Jeremiah also prophesized Hophra's capture by Nebuchadnezzar. Archaeologists have determined that Hophra ruled from 589 to 570 B.C.E. and fought against Babylon.

II Kings 17 — II Kings 19 and Isaiah 37 — II Kings 23:29–34; II Chronicles 35:20–36 — II Kings 23:29–34; II Chronicles 35:20–36

SO

King Hoshea of Israel attempted to form an alliance with a pharaoh the Bible named "So" and to rebel against King Shalmaneser of Assyria, who ruled over Israel. So may have been Pharaoh Osorkon, who archaeologists determine ruled from 727 to 720 B.C.E. and aligned with Israel and other nations against Assyria.

RAMSES II

DEBORAH

DEBORAH
MEANING OF NAME "A bee"
BOOK Judges
KNOWN FOR Prophetess; judge; military leader

Deborah played many roles—prophetess, judge, and military leader. She is best known for winning a major battle against the Canaanites.

Deborah ordered her general Barak to assemble 10,000 soldiers on the hillside of Mount Tabor to do battle with King Jabin's well-equipped and experienced army. Jabin's general Sisera charged with his 900 menacing iron war chariots. They raced down Mount Tabor along the Kishon River to where Deborah waited with her army. Just then, the sky opened up with torrential rains. The Kishon River flooded, sweeping the iron chariots and their drivers under the water. Those chariots that survived the gushing floodwaters got stuck in the mud. All of Sisera's men ran—including Sisera.

Deborah gave the call to attack. Ten thousand Israelites charged to victory. With Deborah's leadership the tide turned on the Canaanites. The Israelites grew stronger and stronger, says Judges 4:24, "until they destroyed King Jabin of Canaan."

BOOK OF JUDGES: Unlike judges today, judges in biblical times did not just preside over legal issues, they were also tribal leaders. The Book of Judges describes the adventures and heroic deeds of 12 major judges as the Israelites settle across the land of Canaan.

Because the Book of Judges describes Israel at the time "before they had a king," we know the author is looking back and that the stories were written much later—except for Judges 5, The Song of Deborah. Scholars believe that the song may have been written close to when the events actually happened as described in Judges.

DEBORAH

HANNAH

HANNAH
MEANING OF NAME "Grace," "merciful"
BOOK I Samuel
KNOWN FOR Samuel's mother; giving up her son to be raised in the Tabernacle

Hannah, who is introduced in I Samuel, was one of two wives of Elkanah, a man from the tribe of Ephraim. The other wife, Peninnah, resented Hannah because of the favoritism Elkanah showed her. Hannah was childless, and Peninnah tormented her, mocking her for not being able to produce sons like Peninnah had.

At Shiloh, the early Israelite center of worship, Hannah prayed at the entrance to the Tabernacle, asking God for a son. She wept while she prayed. In her prayers she promised God she would dedicate her son to him. A priest, Eli, watched from the doorway. He thought Hannah was drunk because only her lips moved in prayer. When Eli confronted Hannah she told him she had been pouring her soul out to God. Eli told her to go, and may God grant her wish. Hannah left overjoyed, thinking Eli's words meant her prayers had been answered.

"Hannah was praying silently; only her lips moved, but her voice was not heard...."
—1 Samuel 1:13

HANNAH PRESENTING HER SON, SAMUEL, TO THE PRIEST ELI

Within a year Hannah gave birth to a son who she named Samuel, which means, "God hears." When Elkanah left to make his yearly sacrifice to God, Hannah said she would not go this time. In I Samuel 1:22 she told Elkanah, "As soon as the child is weaned, I will bring him, that he may appear in the presence of the Lord, and remain there forever."

Once Samuel was old enough, Hannah followed through with her promise to God. She brought Samuel back to the Tabernacle at Shiloh where she had first prayed and asked the priest Eli to keep him and give him a religious education. Every year thereafter, Hannah made a pilgrimage to the Tabernacle to see her son and bring him a new robe she had made herself.

Hannah would go on to have three more sons and two daughters.

PRAYER CUSTOM: In this story, it may seem odd that Eli jumped to the conclusion that Hannah was drunk. At the time, prayers were spoken out loud and sometimes accompanied by wailing. It was rare that people would pray in silence as Hannah was doing.

SAMUEL

When he was a boy, Samuel studied under the high priest Eli. Samuel was an honest and fair judge. He followed God's law and guided the Israelites from living under a system of regional judges for each tribe to having their first king.

SAMUEL **MEANING OF NAME** "God heard" **BOOK** Samuel, Psalms, Jeremiah, Acts of the Apostles, Hebrews **KNOWN FOR** Last of the judges; priest and prophet; chose David to be king as directed by God; anointed Israel's first two kings, Saul and David

KING SAUL

King Saul was a generous king and loved by his people. In I Samuel 15, he fell out of favor with God because he disobeyed God's commands. In the end, Saul neglected his royal duties partly because he was driven into angry revenge by his jealousy of David.

KING SAUL **MEANING OF NAME** "Loaned" **BOOK** Samuel, Acts of the Apostles **KNOWN FOR** First king of Israel; united the 12 tribes; plotted to kill David; fell on his own sword after being wounded in battle with the Philistines

DAVID FELLS GOLIATH.

GOLIATH

In a war against Israel, Goliath, a Philistine giant, laughed at the Israelite soldiers. For 40 days he stood on the battlefield, decked out in full armor, challenging them to send a champion to fight him. Everyone cowered in fear, except for a young shepherd boy named David.

GOLIATH **MEANING OF NAME** "Great" **BOOK** Samuel **KNOWN FOR** The giant from Gath who was felled by a single stone from David's slingshot

MICHAL

"Now Saul's daughter Michal loved David," I Samuel 18:20 tells us. This is the only place in the Bible where a woman is said to love a man. Michal married David and helped him hide from Saul when Saul tried to kill him. Saul then gave Michal to another man. Michal never had any children.

MICHAL **MEANING OF NAME** "Who is like God" **BOOK** Samuel, Chronicles **KNOWN FOR** King Saul's daughter and King David's wife; saved David's life

SAUL, ON THRONE, WITH DAVID DRESSING IN ARMOR

JOAB

David ordered Joab, the lead general in his army, to put one of his soldiers, Uriah, in harm's way on the battlefield because David wanted Uriah killed during the fighting. Joab did not follow David's orders exactly, but Uriah was killed in battle regardless.

JOAB **MEANING OF NAME** "Whose father is God" **BOOK** Samuel, Kings
KNOWN FOR Commander-in-chief of King David's army

MICHAL, IN THE WINDOW, WITH DAVID BELOW

BATHSHEBA, AT RIGHT

BATHSHEBA

Bathsheba was the beloved wife of David and mother of Solomon. When David was old and feeble near the end of his reign, Adonijah, his oldest surviving son from another wife, proclaimed himself king without David's knowledge. In I Kings 1:17–21, Bathsheba warned David that she and Solomon would be harmed if Adonijah were king, and she told David to recall his promise that "Solomon shall succeed me as king." David quickly ordered Solomon to be anointed as king. After David died and Solomon took the throne, he had a second throne brought in and placed on his right for his mother.

BATHSHEBA **MEANING OF NAME** "Daughter of the oath" **BOOK** Samuel, Kings, Psalms
KNOWN FOR Wife of King David; mother of King Solomon

ABIATHAR

In a fit of insane jealousy, Saul killed the priests at Nob, believing they sided with David against him. One priest escaped—Abiathar. Abiathar became David's high priest and advisor. Later, Abiathar did not support David's son Solomon becoming king, so Solomon banished him.

ABIATHAR **MEANING OF NAME** "Father of abundance" **BOOK** Samuel, Chronicles, Kings
KNOWN FOR High priest under King David; banished by Solomon

JEROBOAM

When the northern tribes of Judah separated to form the northern kingdom of Israel, Jeroboam became Israel's first king. Jeroboam built the fortified capital city of Shechem and constructed temples in Bethel and Dan.

JEROBOAM **MEANING OF NAME** "Whose people are many" **BOOK** Kings, Amos, Hosea
KNOWN FOR First king of the northern kingdom of Israel; unsuccessfully plotting to overthrow Solomon; accused of worshipping idols

WARRIORS AND BATTLES OF THE OLD TESTAMENT

The first millennium B.C.E. was a turbulent period in the biblical world. Israel lay between the great warring empires of Assyria and Babylon on one side, and Egypt on the other. The stage was set for conflict as foreign troops marched along Israel's busy trade routes, turning them into battlefields as they went. One after another, the empires pillaged, plundered, and oppressed the Israelites, triggering bloody revolts.

Warfare is vividly described in the Bible. It tells how sword-wielding raiders swooped into a city, defeating the residents, looting and burning the holy temple, and making off with women, children, and livestock.

Among the pages of the Old Testament are stories of brave warriors, hard-fought battles, and the battlefields where they clashed.

BATTLE: LACHISH

The Book of Joshua describes how the Israelites, led by Joshua, won the large fortified city of Lachish, in the kingdom of Judah, with the help of God.

Archaeology: The site of Lachish is in today's Israel. Archaeologists have excavated a ramp built by the Assyrians during their attack on Lachish around 701 B.C.E. The ramp crossed a protective ditch surrounding the city.

WARRIOR: DEBORAH

Deborah, an Israelite prophet and judge, joined Barak, an Israelite military commander, to defeat the wicked Canaanite king Jabin of Hazor, despite his skilled army and 900 chariots.

History: The Canaanites used forges, furnaces for heating metal to shape into weapons and chariot wheels. The Israelites had only primitive slings, clubs, and bows and arrows. But rainy weather helped them: The Canaanites' iron chariot wheels got stuck in the mud.

Joshua 1–11 · Joshua 10 · Judges 4 · Judges 6 · Judges 15:9–15

WARRIOR: JOSHUA

After Moses died, Joshua, Moses' loyal commander, led the Israelites into Canaan. First he had to fight the Canaanites at Jericho. His army trumpeted and shouted so loudly that Jericho's walls fell down.

Archaeology: The archaeological site of ancient Jericho, which lies north of the Dead Sea, is called Tell es-Sultan. The city walls discovered there in the 1950s are the oldest defensive walls found to date; experts believe that earthquakes toppled them.

WARRIOR: GIDEON

Gideon was one of Israel's judges and military leaders, whose army fought against the powerful Midianites and Amalekites. Gideon described the enemy forces as using camels in warfare.

History: Speedy camels would have given the enemy an advantage over the Israelites, who fought on foot. To win, the Israelites used guerilla warfare, a practice of unexpected ambushes to surprise an enemy. It is used around the world today.

WARRIOR: SAMSON

When the Philistines captured the strongman Samson, "the spirit of the Lord rushed on him," and he broke the ropes that bound him. Then, "he found a fresh jawbone of a donkey," and "killed a thousand men."

History: The Israelites were forbidden by the Canaanites to forge modern weapons, so they had to be creative: The jawbone of a donkey was sometimes used as a sturdy club.

BRONZE RELIEF OF ALEXANDER THE GREAT IN BATTLE

BATTLE: JABESH-GILEAD

The Israelite king Saul learned that the leader of the Ammonites had besieged the town of Jabesh-Gilead and demanded the right eye of every citizen as part of their surrender. Furious, Saul persuaded the Israelites to fight the Ammonites.

History: Many battles weren't battles at all, but sieges. Armies camped outside an enemy's city walls showing off their strength. If their demands were met, they left without a fight.

WARRIOR: GOLIATH

In the valley of Elah, the giant Philistine warrior Goliath taunted the Israelite army in his "helmet of bronze" and "coat of mail." Still, he was felled by a rock from the slingshot of the Israelite boy David.

History: In biblical times, a coat of mail, or armor, was made by sewing pieces of metal to a leather apron in a fish-scale pattern. Warriors could move easily, while being protected from swords.

BATTLE: SAMARIA

King Ben-hadad of Aram's army lay siege to Samaria, cutting off the city's supplies. As food grew scarce, it became expensive for citizens to buy food: It cost "eighty shekels of silver" for a donkey's head.

History: During a siege, attackers let no traders bring goods into a city. The attackers waited outside the city walls, while the inhabitants starved. Eventually, they would surrender or die.

BATTLE: MEGIDDO

Pharaoh Neco of Egypt, known as Necho by historians, led his army though the kingdom of Judah to fight the Babylonians. The Judean king Josiah did not want the Egyptians on his land and tried to block them. Josiah was killed and his kingdom captured.

Archaeology: Megiddo's strategic location guarding a narrow pass on a busy trade route in northern Israel made it an ideal battle site. Many archaeologists have said that more battles were fought here than anywhere else on Earth.

SAUL, CENTER, DEFEATING THE AMMONITES AT JABESH-GILEAD

I Samuel 11 | I Samuel 17 | II Samuel 5:8 | II Kings 6:25 | II Kings 23:29 | I Maccabees 1:1–7

WARRIOR: DAVID

After David became king of the Israelites, he led his army to capture Jerusalem from the Jebusites and make it Israel's capital. He ordered his soldiers to attack by coming up through the "water shaft."

History: Archaeologists think it is possible David meant the vertical shaft, or tunnel, inside Jerusalem's walls that was used as a well. Coming up through such a tunnel to surprise residents was guerilla warfare.

WARRIOR: ALEXANDER THE GREAT

Alexander the Great, king of Macedonia, now known as Greece, was undefeated in battle. I Maccabees says, "He fought many battles, conquered strongholds, and put to death the kings of the earth."

History: Historians place Alexander's reign from about 336 to 323 B.C.E. As a brilliant military leader, he moved swiftly and strengthened his ranks with engineers, weapons experts, and a cavalry. He won lands from Greece to India.

DAVID

DAVID
MEANING OF NAME "Darling," "beloved"
BOOK Luke, Samuel, Kings
KNOWN FOR Fighting the giant Goliath; a popular king and a successful warrior; composer of Psalms

Born in Bethlehem, David was the youngest son of Jesse, son of Ruth. He was a shepherd who cared for his father's flock. The first Book of Samuel says, at that time, Israel was ruled by its first king, Saul. When Saul turned his back on God and disobeyed him, God sent the Prophet Samuel to find David. Samuel poured oil on David's head to mark the young shepherd as future king.

The faithless Saul became so tormented by evil spirits that he ordered his servants to find him a musician to soothe his spirits. They brought David, who was a gifted musician on the lyre, a stringed instrument like a small harp. David traveled back and forth—playing for Saul in his palace at Gibeah, outside Jerusalem, and feeding his father's sheep some five miles (8 km) away in Bethlehem.

One day David's father sent him to deliver bread to his brothers who were soldiers in the Israelite army encamped in the valley of Elah. When David arrived at the battlefront, he heard the Philistine giant named Goliath taunting the Israelites. David became so angry that he told Saul he would fight the giant. Despite Saul's pleas not to go because he was too young, David, armed with only a sling, went out to face the giant. According to I Samuel 17:49, David struck Goliath with the first stone, which "sank deep into his forehead, and he fell face down on the ground."

Such a fantastic feat earned David enormous praise and adoration. The attention made Saul extremely jealous, and he threw a spear at David. Saul missed, but that marked the beginning of Saul's devious plots to kill David. To escape Saul, David was forced to hide among outlaws in the Cave of Adullam. During this time he married two women, Ahinoam of Jezreel, and Abigail the widow of Nabal of Carmel.

The battles between the Israelites and the Philistines continued until one at Mount Gilboa, in northern Israel. There, both Saul and his son, Jonathan, were killed.

In II Samuel 2, God tells David to go to Hebron, and there, at 30 years old, David was anointed as king of Judah. From Hebron he ruled for nearly eight years before capturing Jerusalem from the Philistines. David moved the capital to Jerusalem, where he planned to build a temple. In Jerusalem David had several sons and daughters, including Shammua, Shobab, Nathan, Solomon, Ibhar, Elishua, Nepheg, Japhia, Elishama, Eliada, Eliphelet, and Nogah.

After defeating the Philistines, David brought the Ark of the Covenant, which held the Ten Commandments, to Jerusalem amid a great celebration. David longed to build a great temple and permanent home for the Ark, but God did not want a soldier such as David—a man with blood on his hands—to build his sacred house.

On his deathbed, David advised his son Solomon to be a strong and courageous king. Solomon would build God's Temple. David had reigned over Israel for 40 years and was buried in the City of David—which Jerusalem came to be called.

SECRET SCROLLS: Two thousand years ago, Jewish scribes hid their sacred scrolls from the Romans, in caves at Qumran in the Judean Desert near the Dead Sea. The hot, dry desert climate kept the scrolls safe from rotting; the dark caves protected them from the desert sun. Called the Dead Sea Scrolls, they held one of the oldest references to King David: "David, the son of Jesse, was wise...he wrote 3,600 psalms."

SOLOMON

SOLOMON
MEANING OF NAME "Peaceful"
BOOK Samuel, Kings, Chronicles, Proverbs, Song of Songs, Ecclesiastes, Apocrypha
KNOWN FOR Son of David; great wisdom; building the First Temple; king of Israel's Golden Age

Solomon was not next in line to be king after David because he was not the eldest son. As David lay on his deathbed, Solomon's mother, Bathsheba, with the Prophet Nathan, convinced David to name Solomon as his successor. Although Solomon is credited with a wise and just reign, it began on a bloody note. Solomon ordered the execution of rivals to the throne—even his own brother, Adonijah.

Not long after Solomon became king, God appeared to him in a dream, offering to grant a wish. Solomon asked for the ability to tell good from evil, and an understanding mind to govern. God was so pleased that Solomon didn't ask for selfish things like a long life or great wealth that he promised Solomon he would be the wisest human ever—no one before or after would be wiser. Tradition holds that Solomon authored several books of the Bible, among them Proverbs, a collection of rules to live by. Such a collection of rules is known as "wisdom literature."

"God gave Solomon...wisdom...and understanding as vast as the sand on the seashore...."
—I Kings 1:29

Solomon's building projects were extensive, including fulfilling his father's dream of building the First Temple to house the Ark of the Covenant. God had not allowed David to build the Temple because he was a warrior. Solomon's reign was more peaceful. However, all of Solomon's projects—walls with gates, palaces, fortresses, ships—cost a massive amount, so Solomon ordered the people to pay heavy taxes. The tax burden was not distributed fairly, which caused unrest among the tribes. His kingdom began to fracture.

Later, I Kings 11:5 tells how Solomon worshipped idols, which angered God. As punishment God vowed to split Solomon's kingdom in two—Israel and Judah.

SOLOMON

FOREIGN BRIDES: It was not uncommon for rulers to marry foreign princesses, as the Bible says Solomon did. It was a form of diplomacy, forging bonds with neighboring nations.

OMRI, AHAB, JEZEBEL, AHAZIAH

JEZEBEL, AT RIGHT, WITH ELIJAH, AT LEFT, AND AHAB, AT CENTER

OMRI

In the kingdom of Israel, Omri was the commander of King Elah's army and half of the king's chariots. After murdering Elah, he appointed himself king. As king, Omri brought expansion and prosperity to Israel.

OMRI **MEANING OF NAME** "Pupil" **BOOK** Kings **KNOWN FOR** Wicked sixth king of northern kingdom of Israel; commander against Philistines; one of the most powerful rulers of Israel

AHAB

In I Kings 21, God grew angry with King Ahab of Israel because of his evil actions. The Prophet Micaiah predicted that Ahab would die in battle. Although Ahab disguised himself as an ordinary soldier, the prophecy was fulfilled when an arrow struck between the plates of his armor, fatally wounding him. Ahab told the driver of his chariot to prop him up in the chariot to face the enemy until death came.

AHAB **MEANING OF NAME** "Father's brother" **BOOK** Kings **KNOWN FOR** Son of King Omri; evil seventh king of Israel; married Jezebel

JEZEBEL

The arranged marriage of Princess Jezebel of Sidon, in present-day Lebanon, to Prince Ahab of Israel was a diplomatic move to ensure peace between their two kingdoms. Jezebel worshipped the pagan god Baal. She convinced Ahab to allow idols into the kingdom of Israel. This led to both their downfalls. In II Kings 9, she was thrown out the palace window and torn apart by dogs, as the Prophet Elijah had predicted.

JEZEBEL **MEANING OF NAME** "Chaste" **BOOK** Kings **KNOWN FOR** Sidonian princess; wife of Ahab; worshipped Baal; corrupted Israel with idols

AHAZIAH

The son of Ahab and Jezebel, Ahaziah ruled Israel after Ahab's death. In II Kings 1, Ahaziah fell off the balcony of his palace and made the mistake of asking a pagan god if he would recover. This angered God. The Prophet Elijah predicted that Ahaziah would never recover. He died soon after.

AHAZIAH **MEANING OF NAME** "Held by God" **BOOK** Kings **KNOWN FOR** Eighth king of Israel; son of Ahab and Jezebel

AHAB, AT RIGHT, WITH FARMER NABOTH

ELIJAH

ELIJAH
MEANING OF NAME "My God is Yahu"
BOOK Kings, Matthew
KNOWN FOR Performing miracles; prophet

Elijah was a prophet, and his story begins with a prophecy. King Ahab of Israel had been breaking God's law by allowing foreign gods in his kingdom. In I Kings 17, Elijah warned him that as punishment a great drought was coming. Then, according to God's instructions, Elijah hid by the Wadi Cherith east of the Jordan River. There, he could drink water from the wadi, or ravine, and ravens brought Elijah bread and meat, morning and night. When the wadi dried up, God sent Elijah to live with a widow in Zarephath.

As Elijah approached the town gate, he observed the widow gathering sticks to cook the last of her flour into bread. After that last meal, she told Elijah, she and her son would starve. But Elijah assured her that the jar of flour and the jug of olive oil would last until the rains came. Sure enough, they ate well for many months—and the jar and the jug never emptied.

Through God Elijah worked many miracles—he brought the widow's son back to life after a severe illness, he burned soaking wet wood with fire falling from the sky, and he parted the Jordan River. At last, in II Kings 2, he did not die, but ascended into heaven in a fiery chariot pulled by horses made of flames.

KURKH MONOLITH: In 1861, archaeologists discovered two Assyrian stone monuments. One bears an inscription that describes a battle where the Syrian city of Qarqar was destroyed. It contains the name "A-ha-ab-bu Sir-ila-a-a," which many experts believe is a reference to King Ahab of Israel. The inscription claims that Ahab contributed 10,000 soldiers and 2,000 chariots to the Assyrian war effort. Although this particular battle is not mentioned in the Bible, it may prove that King Ahab existed.

ELIJAH ASCENDING TO HEAVEN

JEHORAM, JEHU, NAAMAN, TIGLATH-PILESER III

JEHORAM IN A CHARIOT

JEHORAM OF ISRAEL

King Jehoram of Israel, also known as Joram, joined forces with the king of Judah, Jehoshaphat, to stop a rebellion by Israel's enemy, a tribe descended from Lot called the Moabites. Jehoshaphat's son Jehu shot Jehoram in the back as he fled in his chariot. The arrow pierced Jehoram's heart, and in II Kings 9, Jehu became the next king of Israel.

JEHORAM **MEANING OF NAME** "Exalted" **BOOK** Kings **KNOWN FOR** King of the northern kingdom of Israel; son of Ahab and Jezebel

JEHU OF ISRAEL

Under King Jehu the northern kingdom of Israel became an Assyrian vassal state; that is, Assyria ruled over Israel. The image of King Jehu of Israel kneeling, face to the ground, before King Shalmaneser III of Assyria is carved into a ninth-century B.C.E. limestone monument called the Black Obelisk of Shalmaneser III. It is the only known image of a king of Israel or Judah.

JEHU **MEANING OF NAME** "God is he" **BOOK** Kings **KNOWN FOR** King of the northern kingdom of Israel

NAAMAN

When the Syrian army commander Naaman was infected with leprosy, his wife's slave suggested he go to the Prophet Elisha in Israel for a cure from God. God delivered. Naaman was so grateful that he loaded two mules with dirt from Israel to take back to Syria so he could worship God on Israel's soil.

NAAMAN **MEANING OF NAME** "Pleasantness" **BOOK** Kings **KNOWN FOR** Syrian army commander with leprosy healed by God through the Prophet Elisha

TIGLATH-PILESER III

Also known as King Pul in the Bible, King Tiglath-Pileser III of Assyria in II Kings 15:29 conquered kingdoms and expanded his empire from the Tigris to the Nile—bringing nearly all of the biblical world under his rule. When evil King Ahaz of Judah (see page 50) was attacked by the kings of Aram and Israel, he sent treasures from God's Temple to Tiglath-Pileser, asking him to protect Judah.

TIGLATH-PILESER III **MEANING OF NAME** "My confidence is the son of Esarra" **BOOK** Kings, Chronicles **KNOWN FOR** Ambitious Assyrian king; extraordinary military commander

JEHU KNEELING BEFORE SHALMANESER

MICAH

MICAH
MEANING OF NAME "Who is like God?"
BOOK Micah, Jeremiah, Matthew
KNOWN FOR One of the 12 minor prophets

The Prophet Micah came from a small town in southwest Judah called Moresheth-Gath. Micah prophesied in the eighth century B.C.E. during the reigns of three Judean kings—Jotham, Ahaz, and Hezekiah. Like many prophets, Micah criticized people for their evil deeds and then predicted the destruction of their city as punishment. He prophesied the destruction of Samaria, the capital city of Israel, and Jerusalem, the capital of Judah.

The people of Samaria were to be punished for worshipping false idols. According to II Kings 18:9–10, Samaria was destroyed by the king of Assyria, Shalmaneser V, after a three-year-long siege. The people of Jerusalem were to be punished for dishonesty while conducting business. In Micah I, Micah foretold in detail the destruction of Jerusalem and its Temple. As recorded in II Kings 25:8–21, Jerusalem and the First Temple were destroyed by the Babylonians under King Nebuchadnezzar.

Micah's rural upbringing made him particularly critical of cities and their corrupt leaders and merchants. He condemned them for exploiting the less fortunate through crooked business practices, corrupt government, mistreatment of women and children, robbery, and the injustice of leaders who lived in luxury while the hardworking were often poor. In Micah 6:11, he warned the dishonorable businessmen against cheating by asking them, "Can I tolerate wicked scales and...dishonest weights?"

> ***"I am filled with power, with the spirit of the Lord, and with justice and might...."***
> ***—Micah 3:8***

Micah's prophecies were not all gloom and doom. He painted a vivid picture of a future kingdom where nations lived in peace and security.

MICAH

RURAL HOSPITALITY: In rural villages where there was no inn for travelers, the locals were expected to invite out-of-towners into their homes. Travelers would sit in a central place, such as by the village well or at the village entrance, waiting for an invitation. Word of a stranger's presence traveled quickly in these small populations. The traveler would not have long to wait. Houses were built to be large enough to take in guests along with their animals, and the stranger would soon be welcomed into one.

JONAH

JONAH
MEANING OF NAME "Dove"
BOOK Kings, Jonah, Gospels
KNOWN FOR Prophet; swallowed by a big fish

The Prophet Jonah was the son of Amittai of Gath-hepher. He prophesied during the eighth century B.C.E. when King Jeroboam II ruled Israel. Jonah's story began when God ordered him to go to the Assyrian capital, Nineveh, to foretell its destruction. God was unhappy with its people because of their wicked ways. Jonah was afraid, and instead of obeying God's instructions, he fled.

During his escape he boarded a ship, but God whipped the sea into a storm so furious the ship was close to breaking apart. Jonah admitted to the frightened crew that God was angry with him, and he told them to toss him into the sea. Reluctantly, the crew threw Jonah overboard.

God sent a large fish to swallow Jonah. For three days and nights Jonah stayed in the belly of the fish until the fish vomited him up onto dry land. This time when God told Jonah to go to Nineveh, he went. Jonah told the people they had 40 days to give up their evil ways, and they did. In the end, God spared them.

FISH GATE: The walls around the city of Jerusalem had many gates in them. One gate on the north wall was called the Fish Gate. In the Book of Nehemiah, the governor of Judah, Nehemiah, describes its construction. Fishermen used the Fish Gate to bring their catches in from the Sea of Galilee and the Jordan River. Nehemiah once complained that Phoenician sailors who lived in Jerusalem were selling fish on the Sabbath. Recently, archaeologists sifting through the soil in a building in Jerusalem found the bones of fish from as far away as the Nile River in Egypt.

JONAH

THE MINOR PROPHETS

Prophets served as God's messengers. To get God's message across to the people, prophets used parables, songs, poetry, and plays. At times prophets might also speak to God on behalf of the people. The prophets' writings were connected to specific time periods and served as commentary on social and political problems of their day. In addition to the major prophets—Isaiah, Jeremiah, Ezekiel, and Daniel—there were 12 minor prophets. The most important of those 12 were Hosea, Joel, and Amos.

HOSEA

In his writings in the Book of Hosea, Hosea compared his wife Gomer's unfaithfulness to the people of Israel's unfaithfulness to God. The names of Hosea's three children—Jezreel, "God scatters," Lo-Ruhamah, "not loved," and Lo-Ammi, "not my people,"—reflect God's feelings about Israel at that time.

HOSEA **MEANING OF NAME** "Salvation" **BOOK** Hosea **KNOWN FOR** Minor prophet; preaching that God demands true faith and compassion

AMOS

JOEL

JOEL

Very little is known about Joel, but his prophecies are vivid and detailed. In the Book of Joel, he warns that sinners should repent, because the day will come when the sun turns black and the moon turns to blood. At that time God will pass judgment on all nations.

JOEL **MEANING OF NAME** "To whom Lord is God" **BOOK** Joel **KNOWN FOR** Minor prophet; calling for repentance

AMOS

Amos exposed corruption and hypocrisy, condemning the wealthy who made their gains at the expense of the poor. In the Book of Amos he despised false worship and self-indulgence.

AMOS **MEANING OF NAME** "Burden" **BOOK** Amos **KNOWN FOR** Minor prophet; spreading the message that God is for all people

OBADIAH

In the Book of Obadiah, Obadiah predicted the destruction of Edom, a kingdom south of Judah, as a result of unfriendly feelings between Edom and Judah.

OBADIAH **MEANING OF NAME** "Servant of the Lord" **BOOK** Obadiah **KNOWN FOR** Minor prophet; bitter condemnation of Edom's evils

JONAH

The Prophet Jonah is best known for being swallowed by a large fish and surviving three days in its belly. (See also page 47.)

MICAH

Micah foretold the fall of Samaria and Jerusalem. He scolded the rich for not taking care of the poor. (See also page 46.)

NAHUM

In the Book of Nahum, this prophet foretold the fall of Nineveh, Assyria's capital city.

NAHUM **MEANING OF NAME** "Comforted" **BOOK** Nahum **KNOWN FOR** Minor prophet; promising comfort to God's faithful and vengeance to those who were not

HABAKKUK

Habakkuk in the Book of Habakkuk described the invasion of Judah by the Babylonians and the suffering the Jews would endure.

HABAKKUK **MEANING OF NAME** "Embraced" **BOOK** Habakkuk **KNOWN FOR** Minor prophet; least known prophet

ZEPHANIAH

Despite the fact Zephaniah was of royal descent, he attacked leaders for oppressing the poor and for idol worship. His story is told in the Book of Zephaniah.

ZEPHANIAH **MEANING OF NAME** "God protects" **BOOK** Zephaniah **KNOWN FOR** Minor prophet; preaching that neither power nor wealth will shield from God's judgment

OBADIAH

HAGGAI

Haggai in the Book of Haggai scolded people for living in expensive houses while the Temple lay in ruin after the Babylonians destroyed it.

HAGGAI **MEANING OF NAME** "Festivals" **BOOK** Haggai, Ezra **KNOWN FOR** Minor prophet; called to the Israelites returning from Babylonian captivity to rebuild the Temple

ZECHARIAH

One night Zechariah had a series of eight visions about God's feelings regarding Israel's past, present, and future. He recorded them in the Book of Zechariah.

ZECHARIAH **MEANING OF NAME** "God remembered" **BOOK** Zechariah **KNOWN FOR** Minor prophet; prophesizing the first and second coming of the Messiah

MALACHI

Malachi's prophecies in the Book of Malachi are delivered in a question and answer format. They illustrate God's love for Israel.

MALACHI **MEANING OF NAME** "My messenger" **BOOK** Malachi **KNOWN FOR** Minor prophet; criticizing the priests for not following God's law; praising the virtues of giving

Hoshea

Hoshea, the 19th and last king of the kingdom of Israel, took the throne by assassinating King Pekah. Then the Assyrians defeated Hoshea's army. When Hoshea refused to pay taxes to Assyria, they threw him in prison.

HOSHEA **MEANING OF NAME** "Salvation" **BOOK** Kings **KNOWN FOR** Last king of the kingdom of Israel

Ahaz

King Ahaz of Judah was an evil king who burned incense while worshipping false gods. II Kings 16 tells of one of his "abominable practices" in which Ahaz forced his own son to walk through fire. Ahaz suffered devastating military defeats at the hands of the Assyrians and the Israelites.

AHAZ **MEANING OF NAME** "Possessor" **BOOK** Kings, Chronicles **KNOWN FOR** Evilest king of Judah

AHAZ, AT CENTER

HEZEKIAH

Hezekiah

Hezekiah of Judah repaired and reopened the Temple in Jerusalem, before hosting a two-week Passover feast. Still, tension mounted because Judah was under Assyria's control, and Hezekiah refused to pay tribute to the Assyrian king. Because of his defiance, Hezekiah expected that Assyria would attack Judah and made plans to protect Jerusalem. In case of a siege—in which the attackers would surround the city and not let food or water in—Hezekiah ensured that the city could access the spring of Gihon outside its walls by way of an underground tunnel.

HEZEKIAH **MEANING OF NAME** "The might of God" **BOOK** Kings, Chronicles **KNOWN FOR** King of Judah; sanctified the Temple; healed by God

Sennacherib

King Sennacherib of Assyria surrounded Jerusalem with his army and demanded that King Hezekiah surrender. But, says II Kings 19:35, Sennacherib's siege failed when an angel sent by God struck down 185,000 of his soldiers. Sennacherib returned home, only to be murdered by his sons.

SENNACHERIB **MEANING OF NAME** "Sen has replaced his brothers" **BOOK** Kings, Chronicles **KNOWN FOR** King of Assyria; conqueror

JOSIAH

King Josiah of Judah followed God's law. In II Chronicles 34:19 he destroyed pagan altars and idols, tearing his clothes in despair because his people had not obeyed God's words. When the forces of Pharaoh Necho II of Egypt—named Neco in II Kings—marched through Josiah's kingdom on their way to fight the Babylonians, Josiah attempted to stop them on the plain of Megiddo. A major battle took place, and Necho's archers fatally wounded Josiah as he charged in his chariot. Eventually, in II Kings 24, Babylon invaded Jerusalem and ruled over Judah.

JOSIAH **MEANING OF NAME** "Healed by God" **BOOK** Kings, Chronicles **KNOWN FOR** Becoming king of Judah at age eight; restored the Temple

KING JOSIAH OF JUDAH

JEREMIAH

The Prophet Jeremiah began his ministry in Jerusalem in the 13th year of the reign of King Josiah, around 627 B.C.E. Jeremiah prophesized that the Jews would lose their homeland and scatter and be prosecuted. But one day God would bring them back, settle them safely, and restore their fortunes. Jeremiah argued that the people should focus not on temple worship alone but also on the values of God's law by showing compassion for those less fortunate and having faith in a merciful God.

JEREMIAH **MEANING OF NAME** "Whom God has appointed" **BOOK** Jeremiah, Kings, Chronicles **KNOWN FOR** One of the four major prophets; the weeping prophet

JEREMIAH

JEHOIAKIM

When Jehoiakim was 25 years old, Pharaoh Necho II of Egypt removed Jehoiakim's brother from the throne, and made Jehoiakim king of Judah. In II Kings 24, when the Babylonians attacked Jerusalem, Jehoiakim switched sides. He surrendered and paid tribute to King Nebuchadnezzar of Babylon instead of to Egypt.

JEHOIAKIM **MEANING OF NAME** "Whom God sets up" **BOOK** Kings, Chronicles **KNOWN FOR** Evil king of Judah; pawn between Egypt and Babylon

ZEDEKIAH

Zedekiah was appointed king of Judah by the Babylonian king Nebuchadnezzar. But Zedekiah rebelled, so Nebuchadnezzar laid siege to Jerusalem. According to II Kings 25, when no food was left and the city wall began to fall, Zedekiah tried to escape. His army deserted him, and he was captured by the Babylonians.

ZEDEKIAH **MEANING OF NAME** "Righteousness of God" **BOOK** Kings, Chronicles **KNOWN FOR** Evil last king of Judah; refused to accept God's messages through the Prophet Jeremiah

ISAIAH

ISAIAH
MEANING OF NAME "God saves"
BOOK Isaiah, Kings, Chronicles, Matthew
KNOWN FOR Prophet; held sinners accountable; prophesized the coming of the Messiah

Although the Book of Isaiah speaks of Isaiah as one prophet, it actually may reflect the work of at least three different prophets who many scholars refer to as First Isaiah, Second Isaiah, and Third Isaiah. Their combined work spanned the reigns of four Judean kings: Uzziah, Jotham, Ahaz, and Hezekiah. The prophets' ministry in Jerusalem was during one of Israel's most unstable periods, the eighth century B.C.E. Two centuries earlier, Israel had divided into two nations. Ten northern tribes took the name Israel, while the southern half took the name of its largest tribe, Judah. At the time, Assyria, Israel's neighbor to the north, was a rising power in the biblical world. The Book of Isaiah witnesses Israel's fall to the Assyrians.

"...learn to do good; seek justice, rescue the oppressed, defend the orphan, plead for the widow...."
—Isaiah 1:17

Isaiah's call to become a prophet occurred the year King Uzziah of Judah was stricken with leprosy, around 736 B.C.E. In the Temple in Jerusalem, God appeared to Isaiah in a vision. God was sitting on a throne, wearing a robe, and attended by six-winged angels. Before Isaiah could relay God's holy messages to the people, he needed to be purifed. In Isaiah 6:7 one of the angels touched Isaiah's lips with a live coal from God's altar and said, "Now that this has touched your lips, your guilt has departed and your sin is blotted out." Isaiah was eager to be of service to God. God warned him that his prophecies would not be welcomed by the people, but Isaiah persevered.

In the opening of the Book of Isaiah we are shown the wickedness of Judah. The people may be worshipping God through sacrifice and prayer, but God found their deeds to one another unkind, and they were disrespectful of his laws. He was tired of their festivals and offerings, so he was no longer listening to their prayers. Whether the nation survived or not depended on how the people responded to Isaiah's warnings. The missions of the Isaiahs included preaching justice and charity, scolding sinners and showing them the right path, and advising kings who had abandoned God's ways. The Book of Isaiah speaks about injustices to the poor by the wealthy and the corruption of politicians and priests. The messages come through poems, songs, and short performances often using clever word play.

Four songs, or poems, in Isaiah's writings are known as "The Servant Songs." They describe the suffering of an unnamed servant who God chooses to lead but who is treated horribly by his fellow man. Many Christian scholars believe the suffering servant to be Jesus.

Not all of the messages of the Isaiahs were complaints against the wicked. The words often brought courage and comfort at a time when Judeans feared they would be taken over by the Assyrians. The predictions of Isaiah held promise for a glorious future.

PEACE: In 1979, at the signing ceremony of the peace treaty between Israel and Egypt, three world leaders—(left to right) Egypt's president Anwar Sadat, U.S. president Jimmy Carter, and Israel's prime minister Menachem Begin—quoted words of peace from the Prophet Isaiah.

JUDITH

Judith, a Judean rebel against the Babylon invaders, used her great beauty to charm the Babylonian officer, Holofernes. Judith 12–13 tells how she entertained him at a banquet, and when he had gone to sleep, grabbed his sword and cut off his head.

JUDITH **MEANING OF NAME** "Praised," "Jewess" **BOOK** Judith **KNOWN FOR** Bravery against the enemy; saving her hometown of Bethulia from destruction

HOLOFERNES

Holofernes led Babylonian king Nebuchadnezzar's forces against Israel. When Holofernes conquered a territory he destroyed local gods and government. He insisted the people worship Nebuchadnezzar as the one true god.

HOLOFERNES **MEANING OF NAME** Unknown **BOOK** Judith **KNOWN FOR** Vengeful Assyrian general; beheaded by Judith during the siege of Bethulia

JUDITH

BELSHAZZAR

BELSHAZZAR

When King Nebuchadnezzar of Babylon was forced into exile, he entrusted his son Belshazzar with his throne and his army. In the Book of Daniel, Belshazzar held a feast for a thousand lords and drank from the sacred vessels his father, Nebuchadnezzar, had looted from the Temple in Jerusalem. At the banquet a hand appeared and wrote on the wall. Daniel 5:26 interpreted the words to mean "God has numbered the days of your kingdom and brought it to an end."

BELSHAZZAR **MEANING OF NAME** "Bel protect the king" **BOOK** Daniel **KNOWN FOR** King of Babylon; son of Nebuchadnezzar; seeing a hand writing on the wall at his banquet

DANIEL

Daniel was an honest and hardworking official. His co-workers were jealous of Daniel's honor and love of God. They plotted to remove him from office by tricking King Darius into passing a decree that punished anyone who prayed to anyone but the king. Since the faithful Daniel refused to stop praying to God, he was thrown into a den of lions, where he was expected to be eaten alive. But God sent an angel to shut the lions' mouths, and Daniel survived.

DANIEL **MEANING OF NAME** "God is my judge" **BOOK** Daniel **KNOWN FOR** Major prophet; surviving the lions' den

Cyrus

King Cyrus was the first king of the Persian Empire, which overthrew Babylon, the conquerors of Judah. Cyrus respected the Judean religion and customs, and he encouraged and funded the rebuilding of the Temple in Jerusalem destroyed by the Babylonians. In Ezra 1:4, he proclaimed that Judeans could return home with gifts of "silver and gold...for the house of God..."

CYRUS **MEANING OF NAME** "Sun," "one who bestows care" **BOOK** Chronicles, Ezra, Isaiah, Daniel, Esdras **KNOWN FOR** Expanding the Persian Empire; conqueror; allowing exiles to return to Jerusalem to rebuild the Temple; returning what Nebuchadnezzar had looted from the Temple

Sheshbazzar

Sheshbazzar was a member of Judah's royal family and an exile in Babylon. When King Cyrus decreed the exiles could go home, Sheshbazzar led the first group back to Jerusalem. The Book of Ezra tells how Cyrus entrusted Sheshbazzar with the return of more than 5,000 gold and silver items that Nebuchadnezzar had looted from the Temple.

SHESHBAZZAR **MEANING OF NAME** "Worshipper of fire" **BOOK** Ezra, Esdras **KNOWN FOR** Prince of Judah; leading exiles from captivity in Babylon back to Jerusalem; laid the foundation for the Temple and set up the altar

CYRUS

Ezra

After 70 years of exile in Babylon, the Israelites returned to Jerusalem. In the Book of Ezra, the first group of more than 42,000 people set about rebuilding the Temple. Sixty years later, Ezra led the second group to Jerusalem. As a scribe and priest, he studied God's word. He became a leader in renewing the Israelites' covenant with God.

EZRA **MEANING OF NAME** "God helps" **BOOK** Ezra, Nehemiah **KNOWN FOR** Priest; scribe; leading a large group of Israelites back from exile in Babylon

EZRA

Nehemiah

Nehemiah, whose people had left Jerusalem to be exiled in Babylon, had become cupbearer—an important official—for King Artaxerxes I of Persia. The king allowed Nehemiah to return home to Jerusalem to rebuild the city walls destroyed by fire. Later, Nehemiah became governor of Judah and demanded that all citizens sign a covenant to follow the Law of Moses. This confirmed their heritage as a Jewish nation.

NEHEMIAH **MEANING OF NAME** "God comforts" **BOOK** Ezra, Nehemiah, Maccabees, Esdras **KNOWN FOR** Rebuilding Jerusalem's walls; restoring Jewish law in Judah

Acts of God in the Old Testament

The Bible is filled with God's responses when he is unhappy with the way humans have been behaving—either toward him or one another. When Moses was explaining to the Israelites why they should show obedience to God and God's laws in Deuteronomy 4, he told them that God sent trials and demonstrated power "so that you would acknowledge that the Lord is God; there is no other besides him."

The following are some of the most riveting displays of God's power in the Old Testament, with explanations from today's experts about the possible science and archaeology behind them. The trials are listed in the order they appear in the Bible.

Genesis 7 — Genesis 11 — Genesis 19 — Genesis 19 — Exodus 7–12

The Great Flood

God sent the Great Flood during Noah's time to clear the wicked from Earth and begin again. Only Noah, his family, and two of each kind of creature escaped.

Archaeology: So many cultures have great flood myths that it seems likely a flood may have occurred in ancient times, giving rise to these tales. Archaeologists are searching for evidence of human remains beneath the Black Sea to support the story of a great flood taking place around seven thousand years ago. One theory suggests that the Mediterranean Sea may have swelled until seawater funneled through the narrow Bosporus—a strait, or small body of water connecting two larger bodies of water—and into the Black Sea, flooding the surrounding farmland.

The Tower of Babel

God saw that the people on Earth had become so strong and conceited that they thought they could build a tower that reached heaven. To keep them humble, God jumbled their one language into many so that they could not understand one another. They could no longer build the tower or accomplish anything else together. The tower became known as the Tower of Babel.

Archaeology: The Tower of Babel could have been a ziggurat. These massive flat-topped step pyramids were built all over ancient Mesopotamia and what is now western Iran by the Sumerians, Babylonians, Assyrians, and others.

Destruction of Sodom and Gomorrah

God sent "sulfur and fire" to destroy these two "cities of the Plain," where the people had lost their way and become wicked. Only Lot and his family escaped.

Archaeology: Several clues in the Bible have led experts to believe the "cities of the Plain" could have been located south of the Dead Sea. Excavations in that area revealed two possible sites that date back to the third millennium B.C.E—Bab edh-Dhra and Numeira. Both sites were destroyed by fire around 2300 B.C.E. The ash lay more than a foot (30 cm) deep in places.

Turning Lot's Wife to Salt

Angels from God told Lot's family not to look back as Sodom and Gomorrah were being destroyed, or they would be destroyed, too. Lot's wife ignored the warning, looked back, and turned into a pillar of salt.

Science: Rock formations called sea stacks and pillars of salt, which look much like a woman glancing over her shoulder, stand near the Dead Sea in Israel. Sea stacks are formed over time by erosion. Wind and water chisel away at a large rock until a pillar is all that is left standing.

The Ten Plagues

God sent ten plagues to distress the Egyptian people in order to persuade the Pharaoh to free the Israelites from slavery.

Archaeology: The ten plagues that led to the Israelites' exodus are similar to those retold in an ancient Egyptian poem found on the Ipuwer Papyrus: "Plague is throughout the land," "the river is blood," "grain has perished on every side," "cattle moan," "the land is without light"—all similar to the biblical plagues. The poem dates back to the 19th or 20th century B.C.E., at least a thousand years before the Israelites' exodus.

Red Sea Drowning

The Song of Moses describes in vivid detail how the waters of the Red Sea parted to allow the Israelites to escape from Egypt. After they safely reached the opposite shore, the waters poured back, destroying the Egyptian army before they could capture the Israelites.

Science: Scientists have used computer modeling to replicate a phenomenon known to meteorologists as wind setdown. Wind setdown can create a storm surge that causes shallow waters to pull apart. The name "Red Sea" is *yam suf* in Hebrew, which can also be translated to "sea of reeds." That name might just describe the eastern Nile Delta, where wind setdown is common and could have created a temporary path through the shallow waters many years ago. It's still a theory, but it's not outside the realm of possibility.

Giving Miriam a Leper's Skin

Moses's brother Aaron and sister Miriam turned against Moses because they did not approve of his wife, who was from another tribe called the Cushites. Because of their unkindness, God turned Miriam's skin as white as a leper's.

Science: Having leprosy made a person an outcast in society. Leprosy, now known as Hansen's disease, is rare today but still exists in parts of the world. This bacterial infection causes wounds and makes the skin numb. In advanced cases, fingers and other limbs become crippled. The disease is spread by touching mucus from an infected person's cough or sneeze. For these reasons, people in Moses's time—and throughout history—have stayed away from a person with leprosy.

LOT AND HIS FAMILY ESCAPING SODOM AND GOMORRAH

Exodus 14 | Numbers 12 | Numbers 21

TOWER OF BABEL

Sending Snakes

While wandering in the desert, the Israelites complained to Moses about having too little food and water. This angered God, so he sent fiery snakes with deadly venom to crawl among the people. As the Israelites were bitten, they cried out for God's help. He instructed Moses to make a serpent out of bronze and raise it up on a pole. When people who were bitten looked up at it, they were healed.

Archaeology: In ancient Egyptian, Canaanite, and Mesopotamian cultures, snakes were symbols of the underworld, but also represented life and healing. At the archaeological site of Megiddo and surrounding settlements in today's Israel, experts have found many images of bronze snakes—sometimes held by a god, or decorating temple doors. From reading ancient texts, experts think that the image of a fiery serpent was used by healers as a magic charm to protect people from illness or poisons.

AHASUERUS

King Ahasuerus, the king of Persia descended from Cyrus, is introduced in the Book of Esther, where we are told in Esther 1:1 that he "ruled over one hundred twenty-seven provinces from India to Ethiopia." (Other sources identify Ahasuerus as Xerxes I.) Ahasuerus's chief official, Haman, felt slighted when a Jew refused to bow to him. He then tricked Ahasuerus into giving him permission to destroy all the Jews in his kingdom. To save her people, Ahasuerus's wife, Esther, who was secretly Jewish, at great personal risk convinced the king to allow the Jews to arm and defend themselves. The Jews were saved, and Esther's success is celebrated by the Jewish feast of Purim.

AHASUERUS **MEANING OF NAME** "King" **BOOK** Esther **KNOWN FOR** King of Persia; divorcing his wife, Vashti, and marrying Esther

ARTAXERXES I

When Artaxerxes I, the third son of Ahasuerus, took the throne of Persia, he avenged his father's death by killing the commander of the royal bodyguard and the commander's sons. In the Book of Ezra, Artaxerxes I sent the Jewish priest Ezra to Jerusalem to take charge of the city. He also gave permission to his cupbearer Nehemiah to go to Jerusalem to rebuild the city walls.

ARTAXERXES I **MEANING OF NAME** "Whose rule is through truth" **BOOK** Ezra, Nehemiah **KNOWN FOR** King of Persia who allowed Nehemiah to return to Judah and reestablish Jewish law.

AHASUERUS

VASHTI

VASHTI

During a lavish banquet, King Ahasuerus of Persia summoned his wife Queen Vashti to appear before his guests. He wanted to show off her beauty. She refused, so he divorced her.

VASHTI **MEANING OF NAME** "Beautiful" **BOOK** Esther **KNOWN FOR** Queen of Persia; refusing the king's summons

MEMUCAN

Memucan was one of seven officials who counseled King Ahasuerus on matters of law and custom. Memucan advised King Ahasuerus to find another wife besides Queen Vashti—one who would follow his wishes.

MEMUCAN **MEANING OF NAME** "Impoverished," "to prepare," "certain," "true" **BOOK** Esther **KNOWN FOR** Close adviser to King Ahasuerus

ESTHER

Queen Esther saved the Jewish people from complete destruction. By appearing before her husband King Ahasuerus without first being summoned, Esther risked a punishment of death. However, the king loved her and was pleased to see her. Esther was secretly Jewish. Although the king had ordered the destruction of all Jews at the request of his chief official Haman, he gave Esther the power to fight against the order. He issued a new edict that allowed the Jews to take up arms and protect themselves. When the attackers came, the Jews were ready and overpowered them. Purim, the yearly celebration of the Jews' victory, comes from the Hebrew word *pur,* or lot. Even though Haman cast his pur against the Jews, they survived.

ESTHER **MEANING OF NAME** "A star" **BOOK** Esther **KNOWN FOR** Queen of Persia; saving the Jews from destruction

MORDECAI ON HORSEBACK

HAMAN

Enraged because Esther's relative Mordecai did not bow down to him, King Ahasuerus's chief official Haman had gallows built to hang Mordecai. In addition, Haman convinced King Ahasuerus to order all the Jews in his kingdom destroyed. Esther tricked Haman, and he was hanged from the gallows he had built for Mordecai.

HAMAN **MEANING OF NAME** "Noise," "tumult" **BOOK** Esther **KNOWN FOR** Ahasuerus's chief minister; plotting to kill all the Jews in the Persian Empire

HAMAN

MORDECAI

Mordecai raised his orphaned cousin Esther, treating her like his own daughter. After Esther became queen, Mordecai was given an office in King Ahasuerus's court as one who "sat at the king's gate." From this position Mordecai overheard a plot to assassinate King Ahasuerus and then saved his life by warning him. Later, Mordecai helped prevent Haman's plot to kill the Jews in Persia by getting word to Esther, who in turn told the king. Mordecai was rewarded with a high position, and Haman was executed.

MORDECAI **MEANING OF NAME** "Belonging to Merodach" **BOOK** Esther **KNOWN FOR** Adopting his cousin Esther as his own daughter; helping stop Haman's plot to kill the Jews of Persia

HEGAI

Hegai helped Esther become queen of Persia. The most beautiful women in the kingdom had been chosen to compete for King Ahasuerus's affections, and Hegai was in charge of getting them ready with a whole year of beauty treatments. For six months he treated the women with oil of myrrh and for six months with perfumes and cosmetics. Hegai favored Esther over all the others, giving her special food, seven maids, and the best suite of rooms for the entire year of preparations.

HEGAI **MEANING OF NAME** "Murmur," "meditation" **BOOK** Esther **KNOWN FOR** Being the beauty expert who prepared women to meet King Ahasuerus

ALEXANDER THE GREAT

I Maccabees introduces Alexander, the king of Macedonia, which is now known as Greece. I Maccabees describes how Alexander marched from Macedonia to attack King Darius of Persia and conquer his throne, vastly increasing the Macedonian Empire. Alexander went on to fight battles and to conquer fortified cities until, says I Maccabees 1:3, he had "advanced to the ends of the earth." For the first time, nations were dominated by one culture, the Greek culture (see page 39).

ALEXANDER THE GREAT **MEANING OF NAME** "Warrior" **BOOK** I Maccabees **KNOWN FOR** King of Macedonia; one of the world's greatest conquerors; spreading Greek culture throughout the world

JUDAS MACCABEUS, CENTER

ALEXANDER THE GREAT, CENTER

MATTATHIAS

In I Maccabees, King Antiochus IV, king of the Greek Empire, decreed that Jewish worship was to be stopped. In a village outside Jerusalem, one of the king's officials was making sure the Jews performed pagan rites. A Jewish priest named Mattathias rebelled. He not only refused to participate, he killed another Jewish villager who tried to make a pagan offering. Then Mattathias killed the official as well. This incident set into motion the Maccabean Revolt, which led to Jewish independence from King Antiochus.

MATTATHIAS **MEANING OF NAME** "The gift of the Lord" **BOOK** Maccabees **KNOWN FOR** Priest; ignited the Maccabean Revolt

JUDAS MACCABEUS

The son of Mattathias led the Maccabean Revolt after his father's death. I Maccabees tells how, leading an army much less powerful than the Hellenistic—or Greek—forces, Judas Maccabeus used guerilla warfare. He and his troops silently entered Jerusalem and captured it from within. Once he had secured the city, Judas removed the Hellenistic idols from the Temple. This event is celebrated today during the Jewish festival of Hanukkah.

JUDAS MACCABEUS **MEANING OF NAME** Judas: "praised"; Maccabeus: "hammer" **BOOK** Maccabees **KNOWN FOR** Son of Mattathias and brother of Simon; leader of revolt against Syrians; defeated the Syrians with guerilla warfare; cleansed the Temple

SIMON MACCABEUS

Judas Maccabeus and his brother Jonathan both died at different times during the Maccabean Revolt, leaving the last brother, Simon (also referred to as Simon Thassi), to lead it. Forging a deal with the Hellenistic king Demetrius II in I Maccabees 13, Simon gained Judea's independence.

SIMON **MEANING OF NAME** "He has heard" **BOOK** Maccabees **KNOWN FOR** Son of Mattathias and brother of Judas and Jonathan; forged an agreement to give Judea independence from Hellenistic rule

JOB

JOB
MEANING OF NAME "Persecuted"
BOOK Job, Ezekiel
KNOWN FOR Remaining faithful to God despite repeated testing by Satan

Job was a wealthy man living in the land of Uz. The Book of Job tells his story. Job fathered seven sons and three daughters. His herds of sheep, camels, oxen, and donkeys numbered in the thousands. Job was a good man who obeyed God's laws, and Job 1:8 says that he "turns away from evil."

When God bragged to Satan about his devoted servant Job, Satan told God that it was easy for Job to be faithful when his life was so rich. To prove Job's devotion, God allowed Satan to torment Job as long as he did not kill him in the process. In a matter of minutes, Job found out that he lost everything—his herds, his servants, his children, and his home. And yet Job did not lose his faith.

Satan then inflicted Job with sores all over his body. Still Job did not lose his faith.

Job's three friends, Eliphaz, Bildad, and Zophar, told Job he must have sinned to deserve such misfortune—after all, God punishes the wicked. In Job 38–42, God arrived and spoke from a whirlwind. He told Job his friends were wrong. He restored Job's wealth times two. Job lived 140 years, long enough to have more children and see his children's children.

BOOK OF JOB: This book is an example of wisdom literature, in which stories teach the reader about humankind's virtue and its relationship with God. This type of storytelling was not limited to the Bible, but was common all over the ancient world. The Greek poets Homer and Hesiod wrote poems that are considered wisdom literature.

JOB, WITH LONG WHITE BEARD

NEW TESTAMENT

Introduction

The New Testament is a collection of books focusing on Jesus of Nazareth's life and teachings. It is much shorter than the Old Testament, covering only decades compared to the Old Testament's centuries of history. The name "New Testament" wasn't used until more than a century after Jesus' death. The books of the New Testament can be divided into three groups—the Gospels, the Epistles, and the Book of Revelation.

THE LAST SUPPER

Gospel means "good news." The good news that is spread by the Gospels includes the story of Jesus' birth, ministry, miracles, crucifixion, and resurrection, but is most closely associated with Jesus' message of salvation. The first three Gospels, written by Mark, Matthew, and Luke, tell the same stories with a slightly different viewpoint. Because of their similarity, they are known as the synoptic Gospels. Synoptic means "at one look," indicating that the gospels tell similar versions of the same stories. The Gospel of John differs from the other three. John explores Jesus as the Son of God. After the Gospel of John is a fifth book, called the Acts of the Apostles. It continues the story of the Gospels after Jesus' resurrection and gives a history of the early Christian church.

Epistles means "letters." The missionary Paul of Tarsus wrote many letters to churches all over the Mediterranean to help the new Christians get established. He counseled individual church leaders and resolved specific disputes. Other letters were written by unknown authors addressed to the entire Christian community rather than individual church leaders. These general letters offered hope for Christians suffering from persecution by the Romans and Jews, warned against listening to false teachers, and encouraged the faithful with practical advice.

The last book in the New Testament, the Book of Revelation, is unlike any of the other books. Revelation was written for seven churches in Asia Minor who faced harsh persecution under the Roman emperor Domitian. It describes an apocalyptic vision. "Apocalypse" comes from the Greek word *apokalypsis,* meaning "unveiled." The vision in the Book of Revelation is unveiled through symbols, numbers, and vivid imagery. In it, God, his angels, and Jesus are at war against Satan and his demons—good versus evil. The vision overflows with wild beasts, including six-winged creatures covered in eyes, a pale green horse ridden by Death, swarms of locusts with human faces and scales like armor, angels made of flames, a red dragon with seven heads and ten horns, and beasts rising out of the earth.

Christianity was banned when the New Testament was being written, and many small groups met in secret. There was no main church. The Gospels, Epistles, and even the Book of Revelation served to unify the diverse groups that followed the ideas of Christianity. Great distances often separated church communities, with no local leader well versed in Christian law. The New Testament provided a guiding light for those finding their way into this new faith.

MARY

MARY
MEANING OF NAME The Aramaic name "Maryam" has no clear origin
BOOK John, Luke, Matthew, Acts
KNOWN FOR Mother of Jesus

In a town in Galilee called Nazareth, God sent the angel Gabriel to Mary. Gabriel told Mary that she was favored by God and would give birth to a son she would name Jesus—and that Jesus would be the Son of God. Gabriel went on to tell Mary that her relative, Elizabeth, despite being quite old, was six months pregnant with a son. Rather than doubt Gabriel's word, Mary accepted the news. She was willing to be God's servant.

Mary set out to visit Elizabeth in the hill country. Luke 1 says that when Mary greeted Elizabeth, the baby inside Elizabeth "leaped for joy." Elizabeth knew immediately that Mary was to be the mother of the Son of God. After three months, Mary returned to Nazareth. She was engaged to the carpenter Joseph, and they did not live together yet. When he heard that she was pregnant, he wanted to quietly end the marriage. His plans changed, however, when, in Matthew 1:20–21, an angel appeared to him in a dream and said, "Joseph, son of David, do not be afraid to take Mary as your wife."

"The angel said to her, 'Do not be afraid, Mary, for you have found favor with God.'"
—Luke 1:30

At the time, the Roman governor required everyone in Judea to report to their hometowns to register so that they could be properly taxed. Joseph was a descendant of King David, so his family was required to go to the City of David, or Bethlehem. Even though she was nine months pregnant, Mary had to make the long trip. In Bethlehem, Mary gave birth to Jesus. Then, following the Law of Moses, Mary performed all the responsibilities required of a mother. In Luke 2:21–24, she and Joseph presented Jesus in the Temple of Jerusalem eight days after she had given birth and made an offering of "a pair of turtledoves or two young pigeons."

King Herod, appointed by the Romans to be king of the Jews, had heard that a new king had been born in Bethlehem. Enraged with jealousy, he ordered all male babies aged two and under in the vicinity of Bethlehem to be killed. An angel warned Joseph, so he took Mary and Jesus and fled to Egypt, where they would be safe from Herod's murderous plot. When Herod died, the three returned to their home in Nazareth. Only one event over the next 30 years is mentioned in the Bible. This is when Jesus was 12 years old, and he disappeared during a family visit to Jerusalem. Luke 2:45–49 tells how Mary was frantically searching for her son. When she finally found him, he was teaching scholars and scribes in the Temple, completely surprised that his mother wouldn't think to look there first.

Once Jesus began his ministry, the Bible says little about Mary and Joseph. Joseph probably died during this period because he is never mentioned again. John 2:1 tells us that Mary attended a wedding in Cana where Jesus turned water into wine at her request. Mary is not mentioned again for a year and a half, until she went to the village of Capernaum with Jesus and his disciples.

Mark 3:33–35 suggests that Mary often accompanied Jesus on his travels through the region. John 19:26 gives us Mary's next-to-last appearance. At the foot of the cross Jesus said to her and to John, "Woman, here is your son." Then John took Mary into his home as though she were his own mother. Our last glimpse of Mary is in Acts 1:14 after Jesus ascended into heaven. She was in a room in Jerusalem with her son's disciples, and they were "devoting themselves to prayer." How and where she died is unknown.

YOUNG BRIDE: Although the Bible does not give Mary's specific age, it was not unusual then for a girl to be engaged at 12 or 13 years old.

Angels

In the Bible, angels appear in a variety of forms. Two angels who play significant roles are Gabriel and Michael. Gabriel served as God's messenger, appearing to Mary to tell her that she would give birth to Jesus, the Son of God. Michael, the most powerful archangel, battled evil and led God's armies against Satan's. In the Book of Daniel, Michael is described as a great prince who stands up for God's people.

Over time, some biblical experts have defined angels by the actions they perform in a specific verse. Sometimes angels are messengers. Sometimes they come to the rescue. And sometimes they are deadly as they carry out God's punishments and destruction. Meet the different kinds of angels here. Each category of angel is listed in the order of its appearance in the Bible.

Genesis 3:24; Exodus 25:18–20 — Genesis 19:1–24 — Exodus 12:23; Psalm 78:49, 51 — I Kings 19:4–7 — Isaiah 6:2–7 — Daniel 3:28; Daniel 6:10–22; Psalm 91:11

Cherubim

Cherubim guard God's holiness from the sinfulness of humans. God sent a cherubim with a flaming sword to guard the Garden of Eden after Adam and Eve were expelled.

History/Culture: Early Christian religious paintings, called icons, showed cherubim as having many wings and four faces: eagle, lion, ox, and human. Around 1600 C.E., art of chubby infant boys with wings, called cherubs, based on Greek and Roman mythology, became popular. These are seen today on Valentine's Day decorations.

Avenging Angels

In Genesis, God sent two angels to ensure the destruction of Sodom and Gomorrah. They appeared at Lot's house as two travelers, and Lot invited them in. Other townspeople wanted to harm them, which increased God's anger: He soon rained down sulfur and fire.

History/Culture: It was a custom in the biblical world to open one's door to strangers. Many believed that God sent angels disguised as travelers to make sure people were following God's laws. Therefore, travelers were treated well.

Death Angels

In the tenth plague before the Israelites left Egypt, God sent a being called "the destroyer" to kill all the Egyptian firstborn sons. That angel passed over the Israelite homes, which were marked with lamb's blood.

History/Culture: In the biblical world, firstborn sons were the most valued children because they continued the father's lineage; they also received most of the inheritance. One ancient ritual to protect the home from demons was to sprinkle the doorway with the blood of a slaughtered sheep.

Ministering Angels

Ministering angels provide comfort. When the Prophet Elijah fled into the desert to escape the wicked queen Jezebel, a ministering angel brought him water, baked him a cake on hot stones, and told him to prepare for a long journey.

History/Culture: Early Christians believed that angels walked among them and played a part in their lives. These angels did not have bodies—only minds. They solved problems on a person's behalf.

Seraphim

Called "the burning ones," seraphim engaged in the priestly duties of sacrifice and cleansing. Isaiah told of a seraph who touched his lips with a live coal to cleanse him of sin.

History/Culture: Cleansing or purification rituals—to prepare a person for worship—are found in many religions. Catholics dip their fingertips in holy water and make the sign of the cross. In Japan, a water basin called a *tsukubai* at a holy place allows worshippers to wash their hands and rinse out their mouths.

Guardian Angels

Guardian angels are protectors. One example is the angel who closed the lions' mouths when Daniel was thrown into their den for praying to God instead of to King Darius.

History/Culture: Some early Christians believed everyone was assigned a guardian angel who looked out for them. These companion angels protected you from demons, but if you failed to be worthy, the angel would desert you.

Messenger Angels

The Hebrew word for angel is *mal'ak,* which means "messenger." Angels often worked as messengers of God's word to the people. The angel Gabriel, who is also recognized as an archangel, appeared to Mary to bring her the message that she would give birth to Jesus.

History/Culture: Christians today call Gabriel's message to Mary the Annunciation. In the Middle Ages many artists painted the angel Gabriel—often dressed in white—either descending from heaven, standing, or kneeling before Mary.

Archangels

The word "archangel" comes from the Greek word *archaggelos,* meaning "chief angel." Both Michael and Gabriel appear in the Book of Daniel. Michael is called "the great prince, the protector of your people," and Gabriel helps Daniel understand a vision of the world's end.

History/Culture: Today's religions recognize different archangels. Protestants regard Michael as the only archangel. Judaism and Islam recognize Gabriel and Michael. Catholics accept Gabriel, Michael, and Raphael. Some branches of religion recognize as many as seven archangels.

GABRIEL AND MARY

Daniel 4:17 — Daniel 8:15–17; Luke 1:19, 1:26–30; Matthew 1:20, 2:13 — Daniel 8:15–17; Daniel 12:1; Luke 1:19, 26; Jude 1:9 — Luke 2:10–14 — Revelation 12:7–9

Watchers

Watchers can be good or evil. In a dream, King Nebuchadnezzar of Babylon, who had ruled harshly over the Israelites, saw watchers coming down from heaven to tell him of his doom.

History/Culture: Early Jewish groups studied a religious text that included *The Book of Watchers.* Fragments of this book were found among the Dead Sea Scrolls. The fragments, which date from 150 to 50 B.C.E., tell the story of the fall of the angels from their place in heaven, including some watchers.

Herald Angels

Perhaps the best-known announcement by a herald angel was the proclamation of the birth of Jesus, made to shepherds in a field outside Bethlehem. The herald angel was then joined by "a multitude" of other angels praising God.

History/Culture: The popular Christmas carol "Hark, the Herald Angels Sing" was a slow, serious hymn written in 1739 by the English Methodist minister Charles Wesley. One hundred years later, the German composer Felix Mendelssohn gave it the lively melody we know today.

Fallen Angels

The Book of Revelation describes a war in heaven where Satan, in the form of a dragon, along with his angels who had been "thrown down," engage in battle with the archangel Michael.

History/Culture: The fallen angel Satan has been the subject of art throughout history. In the early 16th century, the Italian artist Raphael painted "St. Michael Vanquishing Satan," in which Michael holds a spear over Satan, who lies facedown on the ground. The painting hangs in the Louvre art museum, in Paris, France.

ELIZABETH

Elizabeth was an older relative of Mary the mother of Jesus. In Luke 1, the angel Gabriel appeared to Elizabeth's husband Zechariah and told him that, despite Elizabeth's advanced age, she would have a son. "You will name him John," said Gabriel, and he will "make ready a people prepared for the Lord." John and Jesus were born six months apart.

ELIZABETH **MEANING OF NAME** "My God is an oath," "my God is abundance"
BOOK Gospels **KNOWN FOR** John the Baptist's mother; Mary's cousin

JOSEPH

A carpenter or skilled worker by trade, Joseph was descended from King David. He became the husband of Mary and was Jesus' father on Earth. Angels appeared to Joseph several times in the Book of Matthew to tell him not to be afraid to marry Mary, to warn him to flee from Bethlehem to Egypt to save Jesus from King Herod's murderous plot, and to tell him it was safe to return home.

JOSEPH **MEANING OF NAME** "He will add" **BOOK** Gospels **KNOWN FOR** David's descendant; Mary's husband; Jesus' earthly father

LEFT TO RIGHT: JOSEPH, JESUS, MARY, SIMEON

SIMEON

The Holy Spirit told the priest Simeon that he would not die until he had seen the Lord's Messiah. Guided by the Holy Spirit, Simeon arrived at the Temple just as Mary and Joseph presented the infant Jesus. In Luke 2:28, Simeon took Jesus in his arms and praised God. Simeon was then prepared to die.

SIMEON **MEANING OF NAME** "He has heard," "he who listens to the word of God"
BOOK Gospels **KNOWN FOR** Blessed the newborn Jesus; first to recognize Jesus as the Messiah

MARRIAGE OF JOSEPH, AT RIGHT, AND MARY, AT LEFT

ANNA

The 84-year-old widow Anna never left the Temple. She worshipped day and night by fasting and praying. Luke 2:38 says that the moment she saw Jesus "she began to praise God" and said this was Jerusalem's redeemer.

ANNA **MEANING OF NAME** "Favor," "grace" **BOOK** Gospels
KNOWN FOR New Testament's only prophetess; second to recognize Jesus as the Messiah

HERODTHE GREAT

HERODTHE GREAT
MEANING OF NAME "Hero-like"
BOOK Matthew
KNOWN FOR Ordering the Massacre of the Innocents; rebuilding of the Temple; one of the greatest builders of the ancient world

King Herod would do anything to keep another king from taking his place. When wise men came to Jerusalem looking for the child who was born to be "King of the Jews," Herod asked where to find the child so that he, too, could pay homage. But in a dream, the wise men were warned not to return to Herod. Infuriated at the wise men, Herod ordered the massacre of all children age two and under, in and around Bethlehem. The deed, called the Massacre of the Infants in Matthew 2:16–18 is also called the Massacre of the Innocents.

Herod would always feel threatened by the popularity of Jesus and his followers. In Matthew 14, Herod imprisoned John the Baptist. He wanted to put John to death but feared doing so because many considered John a prophet. In Acts 12, Herod had John's brother James killed with a sword, and imprisoned Peter.

Not all of Herod's deeds were motivated by jealousy—many were motivated by ego. He was known as one of the greatest builders of the ancient world. The Jewish historian Josephus wrote about Herod's architectural achievements: He built fortresses and new cities throughout Judea, and a port where his ships could be built. In Jerusalem he added a new water system, theater, market, amphitheater, royal palace, and meetinghouse. Most important, he rebuilt Solomon's Temple, which had been destroyed by the Babylonians—a massive undertaking.

Josephus reported that Herod's final illness was extremely painful; later, medical experts likened the symptoms to those for kidney disease. Josephus also wrote that Herod died after a lunar eclipse. He was buried with great pomp.

HEROD

HEROD'S TOMB: After 35 years of searching, in 2007 Israeli archaeologist Ehud Netzer discovered what he believes to be Herod's tomb in Herod's fortified palace called Herodium, on a hilltop at the edge of the Judean Desert. Known by historians and archaeologists as a great builder of the ancient world, Herod constructed Herodium and also rebuilt the Temple in Jerusalem.

JESUS

JESUS
MEANING OF NAME "The Lord is salvation"
BOOK Gospels, Acts
KNOWN FOR Son of God; preached kindness and forgiveness; healed people; performed nature miracles; died for people's sins

According to the Gospels, Jesus was born in Bethlehem, during King Herod's reign, to the humble couple Mary and Joseph of Nazareth. Soon after the birth, in Matthew 2, "wise men from the East" arrived to pay tribute to the new "king of the Jews." Hailing Jesus as king alarmed Herod, who also called himself king of the Jews. He feared competition of any kind and killed his rivals. Fortunately, angels warned Joseph about Herod in a dream, and the family escaped to Egypt, where they remained until Herod died. Then they returned to Nazareth, where Jesus grew up quietly.

When Jesus was about 30 years old, John the Baptist baptized him in the Jordan River, marking the beginning of Jesus' ministry. From there Jesus walked into the nearby rocky desert of Judea to fast and meditate for 40 days and 40 nights.

Following his time in the desert, Jesus traveled the countryside all around the rolling hills of Galilee—today's northern Israel. All four books of the Gospels tell how he taught in synagogues and healed the sick. Jesus used stories that taught lessons, called parables, as well as performed miracles to spread the word—as in Luke 21:31—that the "kingdom of God is near." Crowds began to follow him, listening to his sermons. As their numbers grew, so did the number of those who turned against Jesus. John 10:33 says that some people believed he was blaspheming, or disrespecting God, by saying he was the Son of God.

On the last Sunday of his life, Jesus he rode into Jerusalem on a donkey for the Passover festival. The crowds cheered him and lined his path with cloaks and palm fronds. Merchants bustled about the Temple courtyard carrying out their business. In a rare fit of anger, says Matthew 21:13, Jesus overturned the money changers' tables and said, "My house shall be called a house of prayer, but you are making it a den of robbers."

Jesus and his 12 disciples gathered for the Passover meal, which has become known as the Last Supper. Later that night while praying in an olive grove, Jesus was arrested and taken to the home of the high priest Caiaphas. Caiaphas interrogated him and then condemned him to death, claiming Jesus did not show the proper reverence for God. But the right to execute a person did not belong to the high priest. So after sunrise, Jesus was taken to high court to stand before the Roman governor, Pontius Pilate. Pilate only briefly examined the case against Jesus and then handed him over to be crucified.

Whipped and beaten and spat upon, Jesus was led by Roman soldiers to Mount Calvary, where they nailed him to a cross. When at last he died, an earthquake shook the land, tearing the Temple curtain in two. Joseph of Arimathea wrapped Jesus' body in a linen cloth and laid him in a tomb.

Three days later, visitors to the tomb found it empty. Jesus appeared to his mother Mary and Mary Magdalene and later came into a room where his disciples had gathered. There, relates Matthew 28:20, he comforted them, saying, "I am with you always, to the end of the age."

LOAVES AND FISHES: On the Sea of Galilee's northwest shore is the Church of the Multiplication of the Loaves and Fishes. It honors the miracle in Luke 9:10–17, in which Jesus fed 5,000 hungry people from two fish and five loaves of bread. This mosaic of two fish and a basket of bread in front of the altar has survived since the church was built 1,600 years ago.

Members of the Family Tree of David

Through his father on Earth, Joseph, Jesus was descended from the House of David. This family history is reported at the start of the Gospel of Matthew. The term "had" means "was the father of."

David had Solomon, Solomon had Rehoboam

DAVID Ruled Israel in the tenth century B.C.E.; valiant warrior **MEANING OF NAME** "Beloved" **BOOK** Ruth, Samuel, Matthew

SOLOMON Ruled Israel; known for his wisdom **MEANING OF NAME** "Peaceful" **BOOK** Samuel, Kings, Matthew

The following were kings of Judah:

Rehoboam had Abijah, Abijah had Asaph

REHOBOAM Under Rehoboam's kingship, Israel divided into two kingdoms: Israel and Judah; ruler of Judah **MEANING OF NAME** "He enlarges the people" **BOOK** Kings, Chronicles, Matthew

ABIJAH Stamped out idol worship; righteous king of Judah **MEANING OF NAME** "My father is God," "father of the sea" **BOOK** Samuel, Kings, Chronicles, Matthew

Asaph had Jehoshaphat, Jehoshaphat had Joram [also known as Jehoram]

ASAPH Stamped out idol worship; righteous king of Judah **MEANING OF NAME** "Healer" (possibly) **BOOK** Samuel, Kings, Matthew

JEHOSHAPHAT Cultivated peace and prosperity by fortifying Judah **MEANING OF NAME** "God has judged" **BOOK** Samuel, Kings, Chronicles, Matthew

Joram [Jehoram] had Uzziah, Uzziah had Jotham

JORAM [JEHORAM] Killed his six brothers to ensure his kingship; formed an alliance with Israel through marriage **MEANING OF NAME** "Exalted" **BOOK** Kings, Chronicles, Matthew

UZZIAH Afflicted with leprosy for disobeying God **MEANING OF NAME** "My power is God" **BOOK** Kings, Chronicles, Nehemiah, Isaiah, Hosea, Amos, Matthew

Jotham had Ahaz, Ahaz had Hezekiah

JOTHAM The prophets Isaiah, Hosea, Amos, and Micah advised him **MEANING OF NAME** "God is honest" **BOOK** Kings, Chronicles, Isaiah, Hosea, Micah, Matthew

AHAZ Assyrian puppet; wicked king **MEANING OF NAME** "Possessor" **BOOK** Kings, Chronicles, Matthew

Hezekiah had Manasseh, Manasseh had Amos [not the prophet]

HEZEKIAH Purified and repaired the Temple; fortified Jerusalem against siege **MEANING OF NAME** "The might of God" **BOOK** Kings, Matthew

MANASSEH Ruled 55 years—longest reign of Judah; worshipped idols **MEANING OF NAME** "Causing to forget" **BOOK** Kings, Chronicles, Matthew

Amos had Josiah, Josiah had Jechoniah and his brothers

AMOS Worshipped idols, leading to his assassination **MEANING OF NAME** "Burden" **BOOK** Kings, Chronicles, Jeremiah, Matthew

JOSIAH King at eight years old; righteous king; killed in battle against the Egyptians at Megiddo **MEANING OF NAME** "God healed" **BOOK** Kings, Chronicles

JOSIAH

The following kings and commoners lived through Judah's captivity by the Babylonians. Little is known of many of them outside the list in Matthew. David's line continues up to the birth of Jesus.

Jechoniah Had Salathiel, Salathiel Had Zerubbabel

JECHONIAH [JEHOIACHIN] Captured by Nebuchadnezzar II and brought to Babylon **MEANING OF NAME** "Raised by God" **BOOK** Kings, Chronicles, Jeremiah, Matthew

SALATHIEL [SHEALTIEL] Second king in exile **MEANING OF NAME** "For this child" **BOOK** Chronicles, Ezra, Nehemiah, Haggai, Luke, Esdras, Matthew

Zerubbabel Had Abiud, Abiud Had Eliakim

ZERUBBABEL (KNOWN AS SHESHBAZZAR IN THE BOOK OF EZRA) Leader of Jews returning from Babylonian exile; helped lay the new foundation of the Temple destroyed by Nebuchadnezzar **MEANING OF NAME** Zerubbabel: "seed of Babel"; Sheshbazzar: "worshipper of fire" **BOOK** Ezra, Nehemiah, Esdras

ABIUD Little is known of Abiud, son of Zerubbabel **MEANING OF NAME** "God is glory" **BOOK** Matthew

Eliakim Had Azor, Azor Had Zadok

ELIAKIM (there is a different Eliakim in the Old Testament) Little is known of Eliakim, son of Abiud **MEANING OF NAME** "God will develop" **BOOK** Matthew

AZOR Little is known of Azor, son of Eliakim **MEANING OF NAME** "A helper" **BOOK** Matthew

Zadok Had Achim, Achim Had Eliud

ZADOK (different from Zadok in the Old Testament) Little is known of Zadok, son of Azor **MEANING OF NAME** "Righteous" **BOOK** Matthew

ACHIM Little is known of Achim, son of Zadok **MEANING OF NAME** "He will set up" **BOOK** Matthew

"Thus your [God's] name will be... magnified forever; and the house of your servant David will be established in your presence."
—1 Chronicles 17:24

INFANT JESUS AND JOSEPH

Eliud Had Eleazar, Eleazar Had Matthan

ELIUD Little is known of Eliud, son of Achim **MEANING OF NAME** "God is grandeur" **BOOK** Matthew

ELEAZAR (different from Eleazar in the Old Testament) Little is known of Eleazar, son of Eliud **MEANING OF NAME** "My God has helped" **BOOK** Matthew

Matthan Had Jacob, Jacob Had Joseph, Mary's Husband

MATTHAN Little is known of Matthan, son of Eleazar **MEANING OF NAME** "Gift" **BOOK** Matthew

JACOB Little is known about Jacob, son of Matthan **MEANING OF NAME** "Heel," "grasper," sometimes "may God protect" **BOOK** Matthew

JOSEPH Woodworker in Nazareth; husband to Mary; acted as father to Jesus on Earth **MEANING OF NAME** "Increase" **BOOK** Gospels

JESUS The Son of God, born of Mary; earthly father was Joseph; preached kindness and forgiveness; performed miracles; died for people's sins **MEANING OF NAME** "The Lord is salvation" **BOOK** Gospels, Acts

HERODIAS

John the Baptist criticized Herodias for marrying her ex-husband's brother, Herod Antipas, son of Herod the Great. Furious at John the Baptist for denouncing her marriage, Herodias convinced Herod Antipas to imprison John.

HERODIAS **MEANING OF NAME** "Hero-like" **BOOK** Gospels **KNOWN FOR** Wife of Herod Antipas, who was the son of Herod the Great; telling daughter Salome to ask for John the Baptist's head

SALOME

Herodias's daughter Salome charmed Herod Antipas when she danced for him at a banquet. He was so pleased that he told Salome she had only to ask and he would give her anything. In Mark 6:24, Salome went to her mother and said, "What shall I ask for?" Herodias answered, "The head of John the baptizer." Salome asked for John's head on a platter, and Herod gave it to her.

SALOME **MEANING OF NAME** "Peaceable" **BOOK** Gospels **KNOWN FOR** Daughter of Herodias and stepdaughter of Herod Antipas; asked for John the Baptist's head

TIBERIUS

SALOME

TIBERIUS

Emperor Tiberius of Rome is mentioned only once in Luke 3 as ruling at the same time that Pontius Pilate was governor of Judea and Herod was ruler of Galilee.

TIBERIUS **MEANING OF NAME** "Of the Tiber" **BOOK** Gospels **KNOWN FOR** Roman emperor; great general; Pliny the Elder called him "the gloomiest of men"

LAZARUS

When Jesus arrived in the village of Bethany, possibly east of today's Jerusalem, Lazarus, the brother of Jesus' disciples Mary and Martha, was dead and had been entombed for four days. But when Jesus shouted, "Lazarus, come out!" Lazarus walked out of the tomb still wrapped in his burial cloth.

LAZARUS **MEANING OF NAME** "God helps" **BOOK** Gospels **KNOWN FOR** Brother of Mary and Martha of Bethany; resurrected by Jesus

JOHN THE BAPTIST

JOHN THE BAPTIST
MEANING OF NAME "God has been gracious," "God has shown favor"
BOOK Gospels
KNOWN FOR Disciple of Jesus; prophet; baptizing Jesus

During the reign of King Herod the Great, the angel Gabriel appeared to a priest named Zechariah. Gabriel told Zechariah that he and his wife Elizabeth would have a son and they would name him John. Elizabeth was cousin to Mary, who would become the mother of Jesus. In Luke 1, Mary came to visit Elizabeth and share her joyful news.

When John grew up, he lived in a sparsely settled area of Judea along the Jordan River. Mark 1:6 describes his habits: He wore a rough tunic made from camel's hair with a leather belt tied around his waist, and he ate locusts and wild honey.

John became a well-known prophet. People from all over Judea sought out John to baptize them in the Jordan River, after confessing their sins. The Book of John tells how one day John saw Jesus coming toward him to be baptized, and John announced: "Here is the Lamb of God who takes away the sins of the world!" John did not feel worthy to baptize Jesus, but Jesus insisted. Later John said, "I myself have seen and have testified that this is the Son of God." As John continued his ministry, his central message, as recorded in Matthew 3:2, was "Repent, for the kingdom of heaven has come near."

In the end, his criticism of the marriage of King Herod Antipas, Herod the Great's son, to Herodias caused his death. To please Herodias and Salome, Herod Antipas threw John into prison and then gave the order to behead him.

DEEP DUNGEONS: According to the first-century historian Josephus, John the Baptist was imprisoned and beheaded in the dungeons of the fortress of Machaerus. The isolated fortress located between the Dead Sea and the Jordanian desert was naturally defended by steep cliffs on all sides.

JOHN THE BAPTIST, AT CENTER

Miracles of Jesus

The Gospels of Matthew, Mark, Luke, and John describe miracle after miracle performed by Jesus. Some miracles demonstrate his mastery over nature by calming storms and walking on water. Many more show his compassion not only for the common man but also for the outcasts and the untouchables. He healed people spiritually and physically, and even raised them from the dead. Matthew, Mark, and Luke often wrote about the same experiences, from slightly different perspectives. John takes a different approach in his language and events. The miracles here begin with Jesus' first miracle, noted in John 2, then follow in the order of their earliest mention among all the Gospels. These miracles give insight into history and the customs people followed when praying, celebrating, caring for the sick, and mourning the dead.

John 2:6–10

The Wedding at Cana

Jesus' first miracle was performed during a wedding in Cana, near the Sea of Galilee, which he attended with his mother Mary. When the hosts ran out of wine, Jesus directed the servants to fill six jars with water. The hosts tasted it: The water had become wine. When tasting Jesus' wine, the servant told the bridegroom, "you have kept the good wine until now."

History/Culture: In biblical times, wedding hosts served the best wine first and saved the lesser wine for later.

Mark 1:21–28; Luke 4:31–37

The Evil Spirit

While Jesus was teaching in a synagogue in Capernaum, a man possessed by an evil spirit burst inside, shouting to Jesus, "Have you come to destroy us?" Jesus shouted back, "Be silent, and come out of him!" The evil spirit threw the man to the floor, let out a scream, and left the man.

History/Culture: Some experts think Jesus chose Capernaum as a place to begin his work because it was on the major trade routes going around the Sea of Galilee; word of his teachings could be spread quickly.

Matthew 8:14–17

Peter's Mother-in-Law

When Peter's mother-in-law was burning up with fever, Jesus touched her hand and the fever left her.

History/Culture: In the ancient world Jews believed they would be "unclean," or unfit to worship, if they touched a sick person. In the story, Jesus displayed his power by healing the sick, and he showed compassion by touching them.

Mark 1:40–45; Luke 5:12–16; Matthew 8:1–4

The Leper

After delivering the Sermon on the Mount, Jesus and his followers were walking down the hillside when a leper fell to his knees. "If you choose, you can make me clean," said the leper. Jesus cured him.

History/Culture: In biblical times lepers were cast out of cities and often lived in city dumps where they could scavenge for food. People believed that even touching a leper made you unclean. In the story, when Jesus cured the leper, he also helped the man rejoin society.

Mark 2:1–12; Luke 5:17–26; Matthew 9:1–8

The Paralyzed Man

The crowds gathering to hear Jesus speak in a house in Capernaum were so large that others could not get near the doorway. So four people carrying a paralyzed man climbed up on the roof, removed the roof tiles, and lowered the man down in front of Jesus. Jesus cured him, and the man went home.

History/Culture: Roofs were made by laying reeds across wooden trusses and then covering the reeds with clay. The word for "tiles" used in Luke also can mean "clay."

Mark 3:1–6; Luke 6:6–11; Matthew 12:9–14

The Crippled Man

When Jesus visited the synagogue on the Sabbath, he saw a man with a withered hand. "Stretch out your hand," Jesus said, and the man easily stretched it out, fully healed. The synagogue officials were furious that Jesus had cured a man on the Sabbath.

History/Culture: In biblical times, any action that could be considered work was illegal on the Sabbath in the Jewish culture.

THE OFFICIAL'S SON

In the first year of Jesus' ministry, an official from Capernaum approached Jesus, begging him to come to his home to heal his dying son. Jesus cured the boy from where he stood, miles away from the boy's home.

History/Culture: In biblical times, people believed that disease was caused by sins. Children could become sick because of the sins of their parents. Healing magic was proof of supernatural power.

JESUS, IN RED, RAISING LAZARUS, AT RIGHT

THE FIVE THOUSAND

While Jesus was teaching a crowd of five thousand, the people grew hungry. Jesus took the only food he and his disciples had—five loaves and two fish—and blessed it. The disciples handed it out, fed the five thousand, and had food left over.

History/Culture: Bread had great significance in biblical times. It was the main food of the region, and it was often a person's entire meal. To break bread with someone was to share a meal.

John 4:46–54

Mark 5:1–13; Luke 8:26–33; Matthew 8:28–32

Mark 6:32–44; John 6:1–11, 35; Luke 9:12–16; Matthew 14:13–20

John 11:1–44

Luke 22:49–51

LEGION'S SPIRITS

There was a man who was possessed by so many demons that his name was Legion, meaning "great in number." Jesus cast the evil spirits from the man into a nearby herd of pigs. The pigs stampeded off a cliff and into a lake where they drowned.

History/Culture: Religious law forbids Jews to eat or even raise pigs or any animal with cloven, or split, hooves because they are considered unclean. They are even called *davar acher*, meaning "another thing," rather than "pig."

LAZARUS

Lazarus had been dead for four days when Jesus arrived in Bethany. Jesus went to the cave where Lazarus was entombed. Lazarus's sister Martha warned Jesus that Lazarus would be decaying by now, but Jesus called to Lazarus to come out. He did, still wrapped in his linen grave clothes.

History/Culture: In biblical times, it was the Jewish custom to prepare a body with spices and wrap it in linen.

THE SERVANT'S EAR

The night before Jesus' death, he and his disciples prayed in the Garden of Gethsemane on the Mount of Olives. When the chief priests came to arrest Jesus, one of his followers cut off the ear of the high priest's servant. Jesus healed him.

History/Culture: Gethsemane, which means "olive press," was a place where oil from the mountain's olives was produced. Olive trees are still abundant in the region today. Some trees near Gethsemane could be more than one thousand years old.

SIMON PETER

SIMON PETER
MEANING OF NAME "Rock"
BOOK Gospels, Acts
KNOWN FOR One of the Twelve Apostles; leader of the Christian movement, or Christianity

"And I tell you, you are Peter, and on this rock I will build my church," said Jesus to his apostle Simon in Matthew 16:18. When Jesus called Peter his "rock," he meant that Peter was his closest and most reliable friend—the person he could entrust to carry out his ministry. Peter's original name in the Bible was Simon. After Jesus asked him to become a disciple, he renamed him Peter.

"They even carried out the sick into the streets, and laid them on cots and mats, in order that Peter's shadow might fall on some of them as he came by."
—Acts 5:15

Peter came from a small village on the northeastern shore of the Sea of Galilee called Bethsaida. Bethsaida means "house of fishing," named for the town's main industry. Peter and his brother Andrew were fishermen. The brothers had become followers of John the Baptist. Then, according to John 1:38–41, Andrew met Jesus and told his brother, "We have found the Messiah." In Luke 5:11, we learn that Peter gave up everything to follow Jesus.

Although we know Peter was married, the Bible does not mention his wife. Only Matthew 8:14–15 speaks of his mother-in-law, who lay ill in her home in Capernaum until Jesus healed her. Her home became the headquarters for Jesus' ministry, where the sick and those believed to be possessed by evil spirits came to be healed. Just steps from Peter's mother-in-law's home, in the synagogue of Capernaum, Jesus began teaching. From that point on, Peter became Jesus' right-hand man—his "rock."

Peter was witness to many of Jesus' miracles, including the transfiguration described in Matthew 17, when Jesus appeared as white light "and his face shone like the sun." After Jesus had ascended into heaven, Peter performed miracles of his own, healing the sick and even bringing a woman back to life. But Peter was an imperfect man. Once during a storm, Jesus told Peter to walk across the Sea of Galilee to meet him. Peter became frightened and for a moment lost faith. He sank into the water.

Peter revealed his flawed nature in an even greater way in Mark 14:53–72, when Jesus was arrested for blasphemy and was to be tried before chief priests and elders. Peter followed the officials who had seized Jesus and waited in a courtyard while Jesus was questioned. Villagers in the courtyard recognized Peter as one of Jesus' disciples, but Peter denied knowing Jesus three times. Then Peter remembered Jesus' prophecy that before the rooster crowed twice he would deny Jesus three times. He broke down and cried.

After Jesus' death, Peter traveled to Palestine and beyond. He continued to preach despite beatings and arrests. He considered it an honor to suffer while spreading Jesus' message.

Christian tradition holds that Peter was arrested in Rome, condemned, and crucified. He insisted on being hung upside down because he felt unworthy to die in the same position as Jesus.

SAINT PETER'S TOMB: The burial ground beneath Saint Peter's Basilica in Vatican City, named for Peter the Apostle, is known as the Vatican Necropolis and called the Tomb of the Dead. Even though a tomb is usually for one person, this one holds many. In 1942, while excavating under the basilica in the years following Pope Pius XI's death in 1939, archaeologists discovered a casket and engraving with the Greek words *Petros eni* which means "Peter is here." The remains found inside the casket were placed in a shoebox and stored in an ordinary cupboard by one of the basilica workers. Whether or not these bone fragments are truly the remains of Saint Peter is debated. Today the relics no longer reside in a shoebox, but in an urn, in a private chapel, in the palace of the pope. The pope is the leader of the Catholic Church, which was the first church of Christianity. Catholics honor Saint Peter as the first pope.

The Twelve Apostles

Early in Jesus' ministry he chose 12 disciples to learn from him and spread his teachings. Mark 3:14–15 says that "he appointed twelve, whom he also named apostles, to be with him, and to be sent out to proclaim the message, and to have authority to cast out demons." After Jesus' death, the 12 continued to spread his word through a ministry called Christianity.

Peter

This fisherman, born as Simon, and his brother Andrew were Jesus' first disciples. Peter was Jesus' most trusted friend and would lead Jesus' new ministry after his death. (See pages 78–79.)

PETER **MEANING OF NAME** "Rock" **BOOK** Gospels, Acts **KNOWN FOR** One of the Twelve Apostles; leader of the Christian movement, or Christianity

James, Son of Zebedee [James the Greater]

James, along with John and Peter, was one of three apostles in Jesus' innermost circle. Because of their outspokenness, Jesus called James and his brother John "Sons of thunder." James was the first of the original apostles to be martyred, or put to death, for not renouncing the new Christian faith.

JAMES **MEANING OF NAME** "Supplanter" **BOOK** Gospels **KNOWN FOR** Apostle; witness to Jesus' raising the daughter of Jairus from the dead, the transfiguration, and Jesus' agony in Gethsemane

Judas Iscariot

Manager of the Apostles' finances, Judas was the only Judean, or resident of Judea, among the Apostles. In the end, he betrayed Jesus. (See page 83.)

JUDAS **MEANING OF NAME** "Praise" **BOOK** Gospels, Acts **KNOWN FOR** Betraying Jesus

John

Like his brother James, John was a fisherman who became one of Jesus' closest disciples and was even known as the beloved disciple. According to his own account in John 19:25–27, he stood with Mary—the mother of Jesus—at the base of Jesus' cross, then took her home as his own mother after Jesus died. He produced the Gospel of John. After Jesus' death, he spread Jesus' teachings through parts of Asia.

JOHN **MEANING OF NAME** "God has been gracious," "God has shown favor" **BOOK** Gospels, Acts **KNOWN FOR** Jesus' beloved disciple

Andrew

Andrew brought many disciples to Jesus, including his own brother Peter. John 1:36–42 tells how Andrew had heard John the Baptist speak of Jesus as "the Lamb of God." He told his brother Peter, and they immediately went to where Jesus was staying.

ANDREW **MEANING OF NAME** "Strong man" **BOOK** Gospels, Acts **KNOWN FOR** Jesus' first apostle; Peter's brother; missionary preaching the gospel

ANDREW, AT LEFT, AND THOMAS

BARTHOLOMEW OR NATHANAEL

Nathanael is referred to as Bartholomew in the synoptic Gospels. These are the first three gospels: Matthew, Mark, and Luke, named synoptic for the word "synopsis," or general view. These gospels all take a similar view in telling Jesus' story. Before Nathanael joined Jesus' ministry, Jesus had a vision of Nathanael sitting under a fig tree. Jesus told him in John 1:51 that he "will see heaven opened and the angels of God ascending and descending upon the Son of Man." Some scholars believe he is the only apostle descended from royalty.

BARTHOLOMEW or NATHANAEL **MEANING OF NAME** Bartholomew: "son of Tolmai"; Nathanael: "gift of God" **BOOK** Gospels, Acts **KNOWN FOR** Apostle; missionary; one of the lesser known disciples

JAMES THE LESSER OR THE YOUNGER

James the Lesser is called "lesser" to distinguish him from James, son of Zebedee—James the Greater. In Matthew 10:3 and Mark 3:18, he is called James son of Alphaeus. Also in the Gospel of Mark, Jesus called James up the mountain to appoint him as an apostle and, along with the other apostles, give him the authority to cast out demons.

JAMES **MEANING OF NAME** "Supplanter" **BOOK** Gospels **KNOWN FOR** Apostle; missionary in Palestine and Egypt; one of the little known disciples

THADDAEUS OR JUDAS

Little is known about Thaddaeus. At the last supper the night before Jesus died, he asked Jesus why he did not reveal himself to the world. In the Gospels of Mark and Matthew he is called Thaddaeus. In Luke, John, and Acts he is called Judas, but should not be confused with Judas Iscariot.

THADDAEUS or JUDAS **MEANING OF NAME** Thaddaeus: "heart," "courageous"; Judas: "praise" **BOOK** Gospels, Acts **KNOWN FOR** Apostle; missionary throughout Palestine

MATTHEW

Matthew was a tax collector until Jesus appointed him to be an apostle. He was the first person to write down the teachings of Jesus.

MATTHEW **MEANING OF NAME** "Gift of God" **BOOK** Gospels, Acts **KNOWN FOR** Apostle; detailed record keeper; missionary; Gospel writer

PHILIP

Philip was one of Jesus' earliest followers. In John 6, during the miracle of feeding the crowd of five thousand from two fish and five loaves of bread, Jesus asked Philip where they could get bread to feed the crowd of followers. Philip answered that not even six months' wages would be enough to buy a little bread for each person.

PHILIP **MEANING OF NAME** "Fond of horses" **BOOK** Gospels, Acts (his appearance in Acts is contested) **KNOWN FOR** Apostle; bringing Nathanael to Jesus; his symbol is the basket from his part in the multiplying of bread and fish

SIMON THE ZEALOT

Almost nothing is known about Simon the Zealot. He is only mentioned in Luke 6:15 and the other Gospels as one in a list of the Twelve Apostles.

SIMON **MEANING OF NAME** "God has heard" **BOOK** Gospels, Acts **KNOWN FOR** Apostle; zealous following of God's law

THOMAS

Thomas was not present when Jesus appeared to the Apostles after his resurrection. He did not believe the others when they told him Jesus had risen. The term "doubting thomas" comes from that passage in John 20:25. (See page 87.)

THOMAS **MEANING OF NAME** Called Didymus, meaning "twin" **BOOK** Gospels, Acts **KNOWN FOR** Apostle; doubting Jesus' resurrection

Pontius Pilate

PONTIUS PILATE
MEANING OF NAME "Armed with a spear" (uncertain origin)
BOOK Gospels
KNOWN FOR Cruel Roman governor; sentencing Jesus

Pontius Pilate was the governor of the Roman province made up of Judea, Samaria, and Idumea. He was appointed by and ruled under Emperor Tiberius from 26 to 36 C.E. However, he will always be best known as the governor who ordered Jesus' crucifixion.

Although government officials lived in the administrative center of Caesarea, Pilate made it his business to travel to Jerusalem during festivals to enforce law and order. An account from the historian Josephus tells that Pilate led a small military force to control the crowd and quell any disturbances that arose.

Writings from the period, such as accounts from Jewish philosopher Philo, who lived in Alexandria, depict Pilate as cruel, merciless, spiteful, angry, and stubborn. He was known to execute prisoners without a trial and provoke his Jewish subjects so that he could justify mass killings. The historian Josephus described how he disrespected the Jews by minting coins with pagan images and attempting to abolish Jewish law.

Acts 4:29 speaks of his "threats." But Matthew 27:20–23 says that when Jesus was arrested and brought before Pontius Pilate for trial, Pilate did not immediately condemn Jesus to death. He asked the crowd, "Why, what evil has he done?" But the chief priests and elders, who were jealous of Jesus, persuaded the crowd to call out for Jesus' death. At the crowd's urging, he finally handed Jesus over to be crucified.

In the end Pontius Pilate was removed from office because of his brutality and incompetence. In the accounts of the fourth-century historian Eusebius, Pilate always seemed to be in trouble with Roman officials. Finally, Pilate was deposed and recalled to Rome. There were many legends surrounding his death, including one in which Pilate's corpse was thrown into the Tiber River, releasing evil spirits that created a violent storm.

PONTIUS PILATE, SEATED

THE PILATE STONE: In 1961, archaeologists were excavating a staircase in an ancient Roman sports stadium near Caesarea Maritima, in northern Israel on the Mediterranean coast, when they found an inscribed limestone block. Experts believe the inscription is part of a longer text dedicating a building, perhaps a temple, to the emperor Tiberius. The Pilate Stone, as it is called, mentions Pilate as an official of Judea. It is the only archaeological evidence found to date that proves Pontius Pilate existed.

JUDAS ISCARIOT

JUDAS ISCARIOT
MEANING OF NAME "Praise"
BOOK Gospels, Acts
KNOWN FOR Being an apostle; betraying Jesus

Judas Iscariot was one of the original Twelve Apostles, and the only one not from Galilee. He managed the money for those who traveled with Jesus, arranging and paying for food and lodging from their common funds, or purse. But Judas did not always use the funds as the others would have liked. We learn in John 12:3–6 that he criticized Jesus' follower Mary, sister of Lazarus, for not selling an expensive perfume she poured over Jesus' feet as an offering. He said it should be sold and the proceeds given to the poor. But John states that Judas said this "not because he cared about the poor" but because Judas planned on stealing it for his own use.

According to Luke 22, when Jesus and the Apostles entered Jerusalem to celebrate Passover, Satan entered Judas. Judas then approached the chief priests to see how much money he could get if he told them where to find Jesus. Matthew 26:15 says, "They paid him thirty pieces of silver." To tip off the chief priests as to which disciple was Jesus, Judas told them he would greet Jesus with a kiss, which was a common expression of respect at the time.

"Jesus said to him, 'Judas, is it with a kiss that you are betraying the Son of Man?'"
—Luke 22:48

When Jesus was condemned to death, Judas realized what a terrible thing he had done. He tried to give back the 30 pieces of silver, saying "I have sinned by betraying innocent blood." But it was too late. Throwing the silver onto the Temple's floor, Judas left and hanged himself in despair. The elders used the money to buy a field to bury foreigners. Because of the money's history, says Matthew 27:8, the field came to be called "The Field of Blood."

JUDAS ISCARIOT KISSING JESUS

GOSPEL OF JUDAS: Some experts suggest that Judas's name may have foretold his betrayal of Jesus. Judas Iscariot, or Iskariot, may mean that Judas came from the town of Kerioth in southern Judea. That made him an outsider among Jesus' group of followers, who were mostly from Galilee. Another theory is that the name Iscariot may come from the Latin word *sicarius*, which means "daggerman."

Jesus' Parables

One way Jesus taught his followers was by telling them stories. These stories, or parables, often had an unexpected ending—one designed to make the listener think. To better understand the parables, it helps to understand the ancient world. For example, we now think of a good Samaritan as a person who stops and helps another person. But when Jesus told the parable of the Good Samaritan, his audience did not think of a Samaritan as a good person. In fact, the Jews despised the Samaritans. Knowing that detail gives the parable a deeper meaning. In their Gospels, Matthew and Luke usually wrote about the same events in Jesus' life in similar order. These parables follow Jesus' time as a teacher and are introduced by their earliest appearance in these two Gospels. Find out below how each one is an example of the history and culture of the day.

Luke 10:25–37

The Good Samaritan

A Samaritan helped a Jew who was injured and stranded on the side of the road, even though Jews and Samaritans had despised one another for centuries. Jesus' story gave another example of how they could treat one another.

History/Culture: In the eighth century B.C.E. Assyria captured the Jewish city of Samaria. Many pagans moved in and adopted the Jewish religion; but these new Samaritans also continued to worship idols. The Jews considered this an insult to God's law.

Luke 11:5–13

The Friend at Midnight

A man knocked on his friend's door at midnight asking for bread to feed an unexpected visitor. The friend called out: "The door has already been locked and my children are with me in bed." Jesus explained that the man must be persistent, until the door is opened to him.

History/Culture: In biblical times, it was common for everyone in a family to sleep together on an elevated pallet. The mother and father would sleep on the outsides with their children between them.

Matthew 13:1–23

The Farmer Who Sows His Seeds

The seeds a farmer threw on rich soil grew and produced crops, while the seeds that fell on rocky land did not. Jesus compared the seeds that produced crops to the words of God that were followed. The other seeds were words that were heard but did not take "root."

History/Culture: The soil of Galilee was not always rich for planting. Farmers understood what would happen to seeds that were scattered on rocky land, sun-scorched soil, and among plants that choked them out.

Luke 15:11–32

The Prodigal Son

Jesus told this story to the Pharisees: The son of a wealthy landowner spent all his inheritance, then returned home asking for forgiveness. The father not only forgave the son but showered him with love and gifts.

History/Culture: The Pharisees were Jews who strictly followed Jewish law and were unforgiving when others did not. The parable's ending was a surprise because the Pharisees would expect the son to be punished, not forgiven.

Luke 16:19–31

The Rich Man and Lazarus

The beggar Lazarus lay by a rich man's gate, but he was ignored. When both men died, the angels lifted Lazarus up to Abraham, the patriarch, but the rich man went to hell. The rich man wanted to warn his brothers of their fate, but Abraham said if the words of Moses and the prophets had not convinced them, then the rich man could not either.

History/Culture: Begging in Jerusalem usually took place around holy places, like the Temple, but sometimes beggars sat outside homes where they knew the food was plentiful.

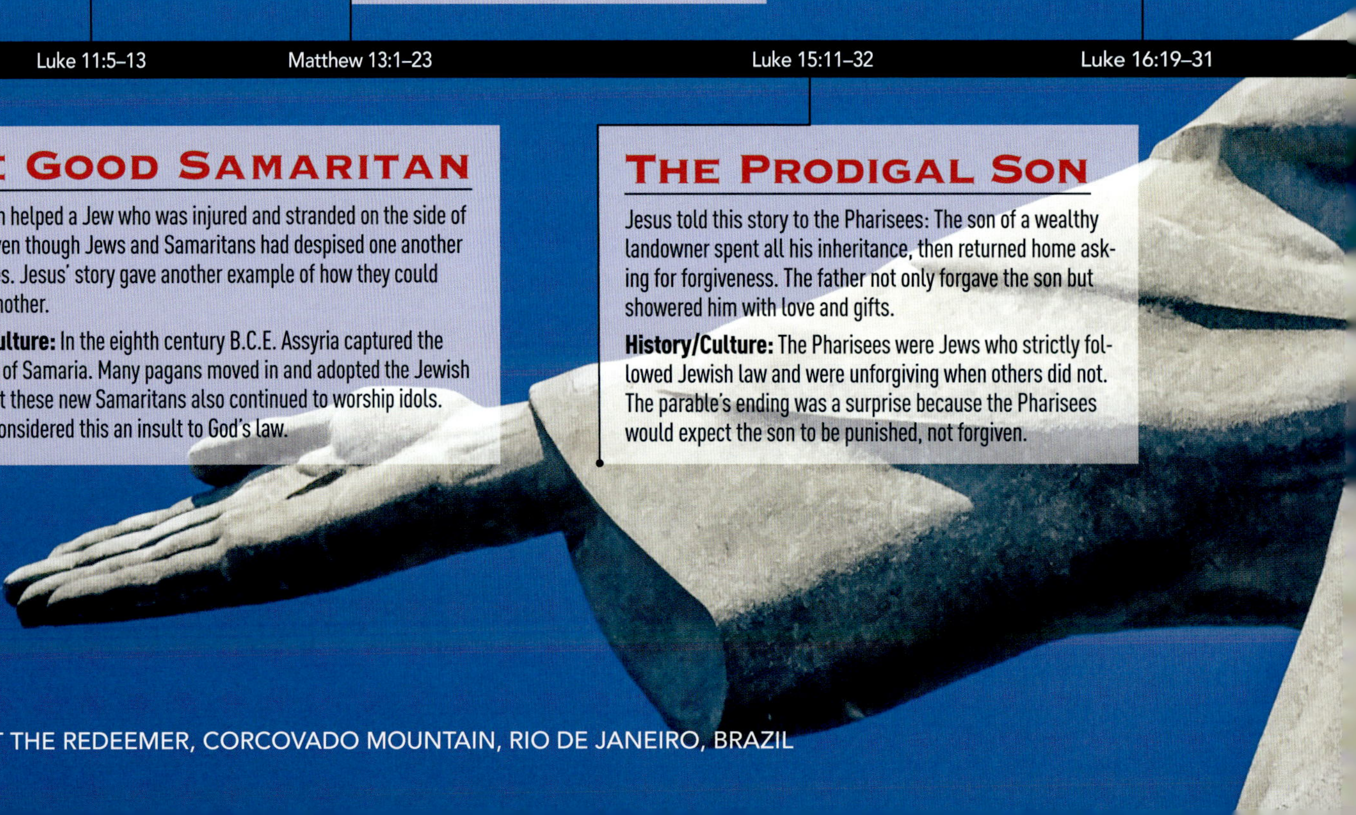

STATUE OF CHRIST THE REDEEMER, CORCOVADO MOUNTAIN, RIO DE JANEIRO, BRAZIL

The Widow and the Unjust Judge

An unfair judge refused to hear a poor widow's plea for justice. Finally, because she kept bothering him, he heard her case and granted her justice. Jesus made the point that God provided justice fairly and quickly no matter who appealed to Him.

History/Culture: In biblical times, judges traveled around Galilee setting up their "courtrooms" in tents. People bribed judges' assistants to get their cases heard. A widow would often be overlooked because she was a woman and might not have money to pay a bribe.

The Unforgiving Servant

A master forgave his servant's large debt of ten thousand talents. But the servant refused to forgive the very small debt a fellow servant owed him. The master was furious and turned the servant he'd forgiven over to officials until his debt was paid.

History/Culture: A talent was a great deal of money in the first century C.E. The common man could work his entire life and not make a talent, which at the time equalled about 75 pounds (34 kg) of silver or gold.

The Wedding Feast

Jesus said not to take the best seat at a wedding; the host may want your seat for a more honored guest. Instead, take the worst seat; the host may ask you to move into a better one. "For all who exalt themselves will be humbled, and those who humble themselves will be exalted."

History/Culture: Weddings in biblical times were elaborate affairs—banquets lasted for days, and longer. Wealthy hosts might even provide wedding clothes for their guests.

Luke 18:1–8 | Luke 18:9–14 | Matthew 18:23–35 | Luke 14:7–11 | Matthew 25:1–13

The Tax Collector

A tax collector and a Pharisee prayed in the temple. The Pharisee proudly told God how he had followed all the rules, while the tax collector asked God for mercy, saying he was a sinner.

History/Culture: In biblical times, Pharisees were highly respected, while Jews who collected taxes for the despised Roman Empire were considered traitors. This tale delivered an unexpected ending when God favored the repentant tax collector over the self-righteous Pharisee.

The Ten Bridesmaids

Ten bridesmaids carried oil lamps as they waited for the bridegroom's late-night arrival. Five had brought extra oil for their lamps, and five had not. When those five left to refill their lamps, the bridegroom arrived. The five with lit lamps led the bridegroom to the party. The unprepared five were locked out.

History/Culture: For a Jewish wedding in the first century C.E., the wedding party and guests would come to the bridegroom's house for a banquet and lock the doors to keep everyone else out.

MARY MAGDALENE

MARY MAGDALENE
MEANING OF NAME Magdala means "tower" in Hebrew; the name in Greek, Trachea, means "fishing" (In Magdala, towers were used for drying fish.) **BOOK** Gospels **KNOWN FOR** One of Jesus' disciples; witness to his crucifixion and burial, and the first to see him after his resurrection

"Magdalene" in Mary's name identifies the place where Mary was born. Magdala was a merchant town on the western coast of the Sea of Galilee known mainly for its shipping industries, as well as its textile and dyeing businesses. Perhaps Mary was connected to those businesses because she was clearly a woman of means, able to follow Jesus and even help finance his missions. Archaeologists have been uncovering the remains of this ancient city and recently discovered a first-century synagogue. Because Magdala is only five miles (8 km) from where Jesus lived in Capernaum, experts believe Jesus must have taught there.

Luke 8:2–3 introduces Mary as one among "some women who had been cured of evil spirits and infirmities." Jesus had cured Mary by casting out the "seven demons" that afflicted her. After this, Mary followed Jesus on his missions as one of his disciples.

"Mary Magdalene came to the tomb and saw that the stone had been removed."
—John 20:1

When the male disciples fled from Jesus during his crucifixion, the women remained. Mary Magdalene stayed through it all, bearing witness to his suffering and his crucifixion, and later she was first to discover his empty tomb. In Matthew 27, she and Jesus' mother Mary watched when Joseph of Arimathea wrapped Jesus in linen and placed him in the tomb. Mary Magdalene returned to the tomb after the Sabbath with spices to anoint Jesus' body, but found Jesus' body gone. An angel told Mary to fear not because Jesus had risen. When Mary brought the news to the Apostles they did not believe her, until Jesus appeared to them soon after.

MARY MAGDALENE AND JESUS

THE MAGDALA STONE: This stone is carved with one of the earliest known images of the Temple Menorah. Archaeologists uncovered the stone in 2009 while excavating the Migdal Synagogue in Magdala. Scholars believe the stone was carved when the Second Temple was still standing, before the Romans destroyed it in 70 C.E. The artist may have been familiar with the temple objects used in worship, and may even have entered the innermost sanctum—the Holy of Holies.

THOMAS

THOMAS
MEANING OF NAME Called Didymus, meaning "twin"
BOOK Gospels, Acts
KNOWN FOR Apostle; doubting Jesus' resurrection

Jesus chose Thomas to be one of his 12 apostles. His first words are spoken in John 11:16, when Jesus asked the Apostles to accompany him to the home of Lazarus, who Jesus planned to raise from the dead. The Apostles were afraid because the home was in a dangerous area where some Jews had tried to stone Jesus. Thomas said, "Let us also go, that we may die with him."

Much later, after Jesus was crucified, Jesus appeared to the Apostles after his resurrection. Thomas was not with the rest, and when they told Thomas that they had seen Jesus, Thomas doubted them. According to John 20:25 he said, "Unless I see the mark of the nails in his hands, and put my finger in the mark of the nails and my hand in his side, I will not believe."

A week later Jesus appeared to the Apostles again, and this time Thomas was present. Jesus told Thomas to put his fingers on the wounds and not to doubt but to believe.

Thomas doubted no more.

"Thomas said, 'Lord, we do not know where you are going. How can we know the way?' Jesus said to him, 'I am the way, and the truth, and the life. No one comes to the Father except through me.'"
—John 14:5,6

JESUS AND THOMAS

GOSPEL OF THOMAS: Archaeologists excavating an ancient Egyptian garbage dump uncovered tattered pages of a manuscript made from papyrus, a water plant. On the pages were sayings by Jesus written in Greek. The papyrus fragments from the third century C.E. claim Jesus dictated the sayings to Thomas. Experts have determined the papyrus pieces contain parts of the Gospel of Thomas. They are known as the Oxyrhynchus Papyri. Fifty years later, in 1945, two Egyptian boys discovered an earthenware vessel while digging for fertilizer. Inside the vessel were 13 leather-bound papyrus books. Among these ancient books, or the Nag Hammadi library as it is known, was the Gospel of Thomas. Early Christian leaders had referred to the Gospel of Thomas, but it never joined the Gospels of Matthew, Mark, Luke, and John. One of Jesus' sayings in the Gospel of Thomas is: "I have cast fire upon the world, and see, I am guarding it until it blazes."

People in Jesus' Final Hours

Jesus spent his last moments of freedom with the Apostles in an olive garden at the foot of the Mount of Olives, also called Gethsemane, meaning "olive press." He confided his sorrow and distress to his three closest friends, Peter, James, and John. After climbing the hill a short distance away from the others, Jesus prayed alone. According to Mark 14:43, the guards came to arrest him, accompanied by "chief priests, the scribes, and the elders." Matthew 26:56 reveals that all the Apostles deserted Jesus and fled. And then, Jesus faced his accusers.

Malchus

Malchus, who only appears in the Gospel of John, was a slave who served the high priests of the Pharisees. When the Pharisees and soldiers were arresting Jesus, the Gospel of John says that Peter cut off Malchus's ear with a sword. Jesus stopped the violence and healed Malchus's ear.

MALCHUS **MEANING OF NAME** "My king" **BOOK** Gospels **KNOWN FOR** Injured during Jesus' arrest; Jesus miraculously healed his ear

PETER AND MALCHUS, IN RED, BOTH BOTTOM RIGHT

Pontius Pilate

The governor of Judea, Pontius Pilate gave the final order to have Jesus crucified. (See page 82.)

PONTIUS PILATE **MEANING OF NAME** "Armed with a spear" (uncertain origin) **BOOK** Gospels **KNOWN FOR** Cruel Roman governor; sentencing Jesus

Barabbas

According to Mark 15:7, Barabbas was a criminal, in prison for murder and insurrection or rising up against the government. During the festival of Passover it was customary to release a prisoner chosen by the crowd. The crowd chose Barabbas over Jesus.

BARABBAS **MEANING OF NAME** "Son of the father" **BOOK** Gospels **KNOWN FOR** Criminal released instead of Jesus

Simon of Cyrene

Simon of Cyrene was coming in from the country for the festival of Passover when the soldiers leading Jesus to the place of crucifixion, called Golgotha, "The Place of the Skull," grabbed him. The soldiers forced Simon to follow Jesus and carry the wooden cross.

SIMON **MEANING OF NAME** "God has heard" **BOOK** Gospels **KNOWN FOR** Man who carried the cross for Jesus

HEROD ANTIPAS

Son of Herod the Great, Herod Antipas had put to death John the Baptist. Later he interrogated Jesus in Jerusalem after Jesus was arrested by the chief priests. Luke 23:11–12 says that "Herod with his soldiers treated [Jesus] with contempt and mocked him; then [Herod] put an elegant robe on [Jesus], and sent him back to Pilate. That same day Herod and Pilate became friends with each other; before this they had been enemies." (See page 69.)

HEROD ANTIPAS **MEANING OF NAME** Herod: "hero-like"; Antipas: "for all, or against all" **BOOK** Gospels **KNOWN FOR** Son of Herod the Great, ordered death of John the Baptist; questioned Jesus before his death

ANNAS

After soldiers tied and arrested Jesus, they first took him to be questioned by the high priest Annas, the father-in-law of the high priest Caiaphas. Not liking Jesus' answers about his disciples and his teachings, Annas sent Jesus to Caiaphas for more questioning.

ANNAS **MEANING OF NAME** "God is gracious" **BOOK** Gospels, Acts **KNOWN FOR** Powerful former high priest; greed; first to question Jesus after arrest

CAIAPHAS

Caiaphas was the high priest of the Sanhedrin, the supreme court of ancient Israel that tried and convicted Jesus. Caiaphas accused Jesus of blasphemy, a crime punishable by death.

CAIAPHAS **MEANING OF NAME** "He will add" **BOOK** Gospels, Acts **KNOWN FOR** High priest of the Sanhedrin; arrested, accused, and tried Jesus

SALOME

Salome was one of Jesus' disciples, who, along with Mary Magdalene, tended to Jesus during his ministry. She was present at Jesus' crucifixion, "watching from a distance" with the other women disciples. Later, she joined Mary Magdalene to visit Jesus' tomb—and found it empty.

SALOME **MEANING OF NAME** "Peacable" **BOOK** Mark **KNOWN FOR** Witnessing the crucifixion; bringing oils to anoint Jesus' body

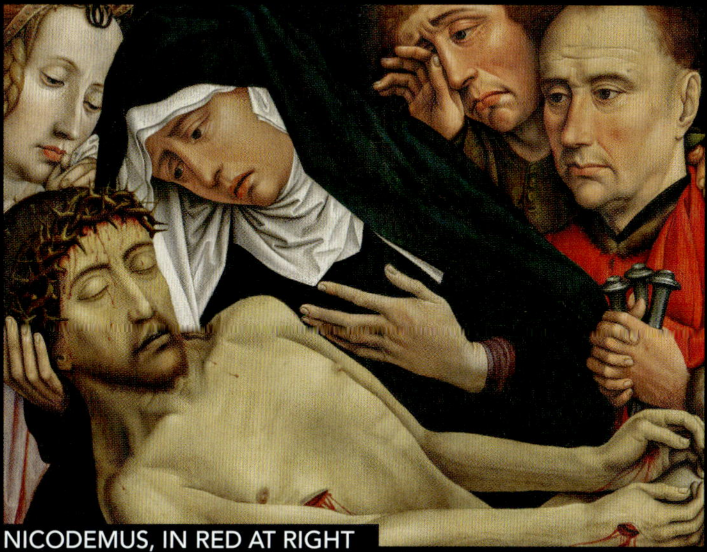

NICODEMUS, IN RED AT RIGHT

CENTURION AT THE CRUCIFIXION

A Roman centurion, or soldier in the Roman army, presided over Jesus' crucifixion. When the earthquake struck, splitting rocks, the centurion was terrified: He now understood that Jesus was God's son.

CENTURION **MEANING OF NAME** "Commander of a century" **BOOK** Gospels **KNOWN FOR** Roman soldier who witnessed Jesus' death

JOSEPH OF ARIMATHEA

Joseph was a follower of Jesus, but he kept it a secret for fear of fellow members of the Sanhedrin. At great personal risk, Joseph asked Pontius Pilate if he could take away Jesus' body after he had died. Joseph, along with Nicodemus, buried Jesus' body according to Jewish custom.

JOSEPH **MEANING OF NAME** "He will add" **BOOK** Gospels **KNOWN FOR** Member of the court that condemned Jesus; gave his new tomb for Jesus' burial

NICODEMUS

Nicodemus brought 100 pounds (45 kg) of myrrh and aloes for preparing Jesus for burial. According to John 19:40, "They took the body of Jesus and wrapped it with the spices in linen cloths, according to the burial customs of the Jews."

NICODEMUS **MEANING OF NAME** "Victory of the people" **BOOK** John **KNOWN FOR** Pharisee; leader of Jews; student of Jesus; helped entomb Jesus

PAUL

PAUL

MEANING OF NAME Saul: "asked for"; Paul: "small," "humble"

BOOK First Thessalonians, First Corinthians and Second Corinthians, Galatians, Philippians, Philemon, Romans

KNOWN FOR Author of many books of the New Testament

Paul was born in Tarsus, today's Turkey. He grew up and went to school in Jerusalem. Paul studied under one of the leading rabbis of the time, Gamaliel. It was important to have a trade to practice in hard times, so Paul learned the craft of tentmaking. When Paul is first introduced in the Bible he is known as Saul. Saul was determined to put an end to the Christian movement. In Acts 8:3, "Saul was ravaging [damaging] the church by entering house after house; dragging out both men and women, he committed them to prison."

On one of Saul's missions to arrest Christians, he was riding to Damascus, a city north of Jerusalem. Suddenly Jesus appeared in a light so bright it blinded Saul. When Saul's sight was restored in Damascus, he had a complete change of heart and was baptized a Christian. Immediately Saul began to preach in synagogues, saying that Jesus was the Son of God. Many Jews were angry at his sudden change, and they plotted to kill him. Often he escaped with the help of the disciples.

"[Paul] went through Syria and Cilicia, strengthening the churches."
—Acts 15:41

For the next 30 years Saul undertook missionary journeys, traveling throughout the biblical world. Acts 13 tells of his first journey, when he converted the magician Elymas by making him temporarily blind. It is during this first journey that Saul also became known as Paul. Having been raised in a devout Jewish family and born a Roman citizen, Paul was able to understand and speak to both audiences. This made him an effective teacher.

During Paul's extensive travels he suffered many hardships. He often went without shelter, sleep, food, water even clothing. Four times Paul was shipwrecked and adrift at sea. He was whipped, beaten, stoned, and left for dead. In Acts 20:23, Paul told the church elders in Ephesus, in today's Turkey, "in every city...imprisonment and persecutions are waiting for me." Rather than feel bad about the torturous treatment, Paul wrote that it made him feel closer to Jesus and strengthened his teaching.

During his journeys Paul wrote letters to churches he had visited and to those he planned on visiting. His letters encouraged Christians to live a good life according to God's law. They contained moral teachings and the principles of Christianity. Paul and his close followers wrote so many letters, they make up more than half of the New Testament.

The last two years of his life, Paul was under house arrest. The Bible is silent about what happened after that. Several historians claim he was tried, convicted, and beheaded by the Romans under Emperor Nero in the 60s C.E. It was during this period, from 64 C.E. until his suicide in 68 C.E., that Nero reportedly persecuted Christians, killing them in arenas using gladiators and wild animals.

PAUL'S DUNGEON: The ancient historian Sallust described one of the most feared prisons of the day—Mamertime Prison—as "disgusting and vile by reason of the filth, the darkness and the stench." Many prisoners did not survive the wretched conditions, and their bodies were tossed into the city sewer. Tradition holds that Emperor Nero incarcerated the apostles Peter and Paul in this underground pit while they awaited execution. The Apostles miraculously caused a spring to gush from the prison floor, providing water to baptize fellow prisoners and even guards. Today an upside-down cross graces an altar in the lower chamber as a memorial to Peter's upside-down crucifixion. Acts 28:30, however, states that Paul lived in Rome "two years at his own expense and welcomed all who came to him"—a far more comfortable life than in a dungeon.

Glossary

A

Ancestor A person in someone's family from an earlier time

Anoint To smear oil (usually on a person's forehead) in a religious ceremony, dedicating the person to God

Apostle One who is sent out to spread the word of God; the Twelve Apostles were the main disciples, or students, of Jesus

Aramaic Language of the Arameans, an ancient people who came from Syria; one of the first languages of the written Bible; Jesus probably spoke it

Archaeologist Someone who studies the history of the earliest people by examining tools, bones, and other items left behind

Ark of the Covenant A chest containing the tablets on which the Ten Commandments were written

Assyrians An ancient people of Mesopotamia who defeated the northern kingdom of Israel in 722 B.C.E.

B

Babylonians An ancient people from central-southern Mesopotamia who besieged Jerusalem and began to exile the Jews in 597 B.C.E.

B.C.E. Meaning "Before the Common Era," it is usually used for dates before the birth of Christ

Besiege To surround a city with soldiers in order to force surrender

Birthright Special privileges given to the oldest child

Blasphemy Speaking about God in a disrespectful way

Books of the Bible The major sections that make up the Bible, often named after events, peoples, prophets, kings, or apostles

C

Canaanites Citizens of Canaan, in the area of today's Israel, where Moses took the Israelites after leaving Egypt

Carpenter In biblical times, someone who worked with stone or copper and sometimes also in wood

C.E. Meaning "Common Era" and generally used for dates after the birth of Christ

Census The official counting of the number of people in a country

Chariot A carriage pulled by horses and used by warriors in early battles

Cherubim A heavenly being; one guarded the gate to Eden after Adam and Eve were turned out

D

Deathbed blessing A blessing given to the oldest son by a father who is about to die

Descendant Someone who has come from a particular family

Disciple Someone who believes and helps spread the teaching of another; a follower of Jesus; the 12 main disciples chosen to spread Jesus' message were called apostles

Dome of the Rock A Muslim shrine built over the site of Solomon's Temple

E

Executed To be put to death for disobeying the law

Exile A period during which a person is forced to live away from home

Exodus A situation in which many people leave their home at the same time; for instance, the Israelites made an exodus from Egypt

F

Fertile Crescent A crescent-shaped region of farmland stretching from ancient Egypt to Mesopotamia (today's Iraq)

G

Generation The average length of time between the birth of parents and the birth of their children

Guerilla warfare A form of warfare in which armies fight by hiding and surprising the enemy rather than marching into battle

Gospels The first four books of the New Testament

H

Herodium The palace-fortress of King Herod, outside Jerusalem

Hittites Ancient people of Anatolia (today's Turkey) and neighbors of Israel since the time of Abraham

I

Idol An image of a false god

Incense A pleasant-smelling substance often burned in religious ceremonies

Inscribed To be written into or carved into

Insurrection An uprising by people against their rulers

Interrogate To question harshly

J

Judah The new kingdom created when Israel was divided into two after Solomon's death

Judge In the Bible, a decision-maker in a court of law and also a military leader

L

Law of Moses The Torah, or first five books of the Hebrew Bible, believed to have been written by Moses

Leprosy A disease that affects skin coloration and the nerves; sufferers are called lepers

M

Manna Honeyed wafers God sent to feed Moses and the Israelites in the desert

Menorah A sacred candelabrum, with seven branches, used in the Temple of Jerusalem

Mesopotamia Considered the Western World's earliest civilization, it covered today's Middle Eastern countries of Iraq, Syria, and Turkey

Messiah The expected king and deliverer of the Jewish people

Ministry Bringing religious teachings to people

Miracle A surprising event that can't be explained by natural or scientific laws and is attributed to God's work

Monolith A single upright block of stone

N

Nile Delta Area where the Nile River empties into the Mediterranean Sea

Nineveh Capital of ancient Assyria, built by King Sennacherib

O

Obelisk A tall stone pillar, usually with a pyramid shape at the top

Offering Something that is given to God as a gift

P

Papyrus A grassy marsh plant used for making paperlike material

Parable A simple story to teach a lesson

Patriarch The oldest male head of the family

Pharaoh A ruler of ancient Egypt

Philistines An ancient people who lived along the Mediterranean coast near Israel; archenemies of Israel

Prodigal Wasteful

Promised Land The land God promised to the descendants of Abraham; once called Canaan, it lay on the Mediterranean Sea, near today's Israel

Prophet Someone who delivers messages, omens, or warnings that are believed to come from God

Protestants Members of a religion that is a form of Christianity

Proverb A saying that gives a truth or piece of advice

R

Relief A sculpture carved into a wall

Replicate To make an exact copy of an object or event, usually smaller in scale

Resurrection The rising of Christ from the dead

Romans Citizens of ancient Rome; they occupied much of the Mediterranean Coast

S

Sabbath The day of rest and worship, as God intended; among Jews it is celebrated from Friday evening to Saturday evening

Samaritan A stranger from Samaria, shunned by the people of Israel; today it means one who helps a person in need

Scroll Rolled up paper or leather or parchment, made from sheepskin or goatskin, with writing on it

Seraphim Angels of high rank who helped carry out priestly duties of sacrifice and cleansing

Strait A riverlike body of water connecting two larger bodies of water, like the Straits of Bosporus, which connects the Mediterranean and Black Seas

Sumer The first civilization in Mesopotamia with a complex city; residents were called Sumerians

Synagogue A building used for Jewish religious services

T

Tell (or Tel) A hill created by many generations of people living and building in one spot

W

Wadi A dry riverbed that fills with water only during rain

Wisdom literature A collection of stories and rules to live by, sometimes including proverbs

Z

Ziggurat A massive templelike structure built in ancient Mesopotamia

Index

CREDITS

Cover: (BACKGROUND), buburuzaproductions/Getty Images; (UP LE), kavunchik/Getty Images; (UP CTR), Neale Cousland/Shutterstock; (LO LE), Avalon Studio/Getty Images; (LO RT), Azoor Photo/Alamy Stock Photo

Back Cover: (UP LE), digitalimagination/Getty Images; (UP CTR), Peter V. Bianchi/National Geographic Image Collection

2–3, Noah Entering the Ark (oil on panel), Jordaens, Hans III (1595–1643/44)/Private Collection/Haldane Fine Art/Bridgeman Images; 4, Renata Sedmakova/Shutterstock; 5 (BACKGROUND), Scott Hailstone/Getty Images; 6, Sir Peter Paul Rubens, Ailsa Mellon Bruce Fund, image courtesy National Gallery of Art, Washington; 7, 10–11, (BACKGROUND), Scott Hailstone/Getty Images; 11 (UP), Renata Sedmakova/Shutterstock; 12, bildagentur-online/uig/Getty Images; 14 (UP), patio/Shutterstock; 14 (LO), Culture Club/Getty Images; 15 (UP), Fine Art Images/Heritage Images/Getty Images; 15 (LO), Zvonimir Atletic/Shutterstock; 16, The Advertising Archives/Alamy Stock Photo; 17 (CTR RT), joyart/Shutterstock; 18, Artepics/Alamy Stock Photo; 19 (LO), John R. McDermott/National Geographic Image Collection; 20 (LO), Culture Club/Getty Images; 21 (UP), bildagentur-online/uig/Getty Images; 21 (LO), Alexandra Lande/Shutterstock; 22 (UP), Lise Pearson/Alamy Stock Photo; 23 (UP), PHAS/UIG/Getty Images; 23 (LO), Jacob and Joseph's Coat, 1871 (panel), Brown, Ford Madox (1821–93)/Private Collection/Photo © Agnew's, London/Bridgeman Images; 24–25 (BACKGROUND), PhotoStock-Israel/Getty Images; 25 (UP LE), James Jacques Joseph Tissot, Joseph Interprets Pharoah's Dream, The Jewish Museum, New York; 26, Culture Club/Getty Images; 28 (LO), bildagentur-online/uig/Getty Images; 28 (UP RT), Lebrecht Music and Arts Photo Library/Alamy Stock Photo; 29 (UP), Culture Club/Getty Images; 30 (UP), Peter Popov Cpp/Shutterstock; 30 (LO), Culture Club/Getty Images; 31 (UP), Peter V. Bianchi/National Geographic Image Collection; 31 (LO), Culture Club/Getty Images; 32–33 (BACKGROUND), Kanwal Sandhu/Getty Images; 32 (LO), De Agostini Picture Library/A. Dagli Orti/Bridgeman Images; 33 (UP), Fred de Noyelle/Getty Images; 33 (LO), O. Louis Mazzatenta/Getty Images; 34 (LO), Culture Club/Getty Images; 35 (UP), Art Directors & TRIP/Alamy Stock Photo; 36 (LO LE), SuperStock/Getty Images; 36 (UP RT), Culture Club/Getty Images; 37 (LO LE), Lebrecht Music and Arts Photo Library/Alamy Stock Photo; 37 (UP RT), Classic Image/Alamy Stock Photo; 38–39 (BACKGROUND), Brigida Soriano/Shutterstock; 39 (RT), Chronicle/Alamy Stock Photo; 40, David by Lorenzo Monaco (Piero di Giovanni), Gwynne Andrews and Marquand Funds, and Gift of Mrs. Ralph J. Hines, by exchange, 1965, Metropolitan Museum of Art; 41 (LO), Lerner Vadim/Shutterstock; 42 (UP), Simeon Solomon, Gift of William B. O'Neal, image courtesy National Gallery of Art, Washington; 42 (LO), Frans Francken the Younger, The Idolatry of Solomon, Digital image courtesy of the J. Paul Getty Museum's Open Content Program; 43 (UP), Renata Sedmakova/Shutterstock; 43 (LO), Universal History Archive/UIG via Getty Images; 44 (LO), SuperStock/Getty Images; 45 (UP), Jan Luyken, Joram, courtesy of Rijksmuseum; 45 (LO), Pantheon Studios, Inc.; 46 (RT), jorisvo/Shutterstock; 47 (LO), Culture Club/Getty Images; 48 (LE), jorisvo/Shutterstock; 48 (RT), Renata Sedmakova/Shutterstock; 49 (UP RT), Fine Art Images/Heritage Images/Getty Images; 50 (LO), Jan Snellinck, Jotham, Ahaz and Hezekiah, courtesy of Rijksmuseum; 50 (UP), Hippolyte Flandrin, Hezekiah, King of Judah, Van Day Truex Fund, 1985, Metropolitan Museum of Art; 51 (LO), Rembrandt Harmensz van Rijn, Jeremiah Lamenting the Destruction of Jerusalem, courtesy of Rijksmuseum; 51 (UP), Culture Club/Getty Images; 52, James Jacques Joseph Tissot, Isaiah, The Jewish Museum, New York; 53 (LO), Wally McNamee/Corbis via Getty Images; 54 (LO), Massimo Stanzione, Judith with the Head of Holofernes, Gift of Edward W. Carter, 1959, Metropolitan Museum of Art; 54 (UP), Photo by VCG Wilson/Corbis via Getty Images; 55 (LO), Culture Club/Getty Images; 55 (UP), Rembrandt Harmensz van Rijn, Daniel and Cyrus before the Idol Bel, Digital image courtesy of the J. Paul Getty Museum's Open Content Program; 56–57 (BACKGROUND), Rocksweeper/Shutterstock; 57 (UP), PHAS/UIG via Getty Images; 57 (LO), jorisvo/Shutterstock; 58 (LO), Aert de Gelder, The Banquet of Ahasuerus, Digital image courtesy of the J. Paul Getty Museum's Open Content Program; 58 (UP), Nicku/Shutterstock; 59 (LO), PHAS/UIG via Getty Images; 59 (UP), Jean François de Troy, The Triumph of Mordecai, Gift of J. Pierpont Morgan, 1906, Metropolitan Museum of Art; 60 (LE), Placido Costanzi, Alexander the Great Founding Alexandria, The Walters Art Museum, Baltimore; 60 (RT), PHAS/UIG via Getty Images; 61 (LO), James Jacques Joseph Tissot, Job and His Family, The Jewish Museum, NY; 62–63 (BACKGROUND), Scott Hailstone/Getty Images; 63 (UP), Leemage/Corbis via Getty Images; 64, Titian, Madonna and Child, The Jules Bache Collection, 1949, Metropolitan Museum of Art; 66–67 (BACKGROUND), nadtytok/Shutterstock; 67 (UP), Luca Giordano, The Annunciation, Gift of Mr. and Mrs. Charles Wrightsman, 1973, Metropolitan Museum of Art; 68 (LO), Marriage of Mary and Joseph, courtesy of Rijksmuseum; 68 (UP), DEA/G. CIGOLINI/Getty Images; 69, Herod Enthroned, Digital image courtesy of the J. Paul Getty Museum's Open Content Program; 70, Andrea Solario, Christ Blessing, From the Collection of James Stillman, Gift of Dr. Ernest G. Stillman, 1922, Metropolitan Museum of Art; 71 (LO RT), repistu/Getty Images; 72 (LO), SeM/UIG via Getty Images; 73 (UP RT), Zvonimir Atletic/Shutterstock; 74 (UP), Matthäus Merian the Elder, Emperor Tiberius on Horseback, The Elisha Whittelsey Collection, The Elisha Whittelsey Fund, 1951, Metropolitan Museum of Art; 74 (LO), Jan Adam Kruseman, Salome with the Head of John the Baptist on a Dish, courtesy of Rijksmuseum; 75 (LO), Workshop of Francesco Granacci, Saint John the Baptist Bearing Witness, Purchase, Gwynne Andrews, Harris Brisbane Dick, Dodge, Fletcher, and Rogers Funds, funds from various donors, Ella Morris de Peyster Gift, Mrs. Donald Oenslager Gift, and Gifts in memory of Robert Lehman, 1970, Metropolitan Museum of Art; 76–77 (BACKGROUND), Lokibaho/Getty Images; 77 (UP), Peter Paul Rubens (copy after), Raising of Lazarus, courtesy of Rijksmuseum; 78, Studio of Sir Peter Paul Rubens, Timken Collection, image courtesy National Gallery of Art, Washington; 80 (LO), Fine Art Images/Heritage Images/Getty Images; 82 (RT), Ludwig Schongauer, Christ before Pilate, The Jack and Belle Linsky Collection, 1982, Metropolitan Museum of Art; 83 (RT), Danita Delimont/Getty Images; 84–85, DnDavis/Shutterstock; 86, Culture Club/Getty Images; 87 (RT), Renata Sedmakova/Shutterstock; 88 (LO), The Betrayal, Cretan School (wall painting), Byzantine (16th century)/Church of the Transfiguration of the Saviour, Paleochorio, Cyprus/Sonia Halliday Photographs/Bridgeman Images; 89 (UP RT), Colijn de Coter, The Lamentation of Christ, courtesy of Rijksmuseum; 90, Karel Dujardin, St Paul Healing the Cripple at Lystra, courtesy of Rijksmuseum

Since 1888, the National Geographic Society has funded more than 12,000 research, exploration, and preservation projects around the world. The Society receives funds from National Geographic Partners LLC, funded in part by your purchase. A portion of the proceeds from this book supports this vital work. To learn more, visit natgeo.com/info.

For more information, visit nationalgeographic.com, call 1-800-647-5463, or write to the following address:
National Geographic Partners
1145 17th Street N.W.
Washington, D.C. 20036-4688 U.S.A.

Visit us online at nationalgeographic.com/books

For librarians and teachers: ngchildrensbooks.org

More for kids from National Geographic: kids.nationalgeographic.com

For information about special discounts for bulk purchases, please contact National Geographic Books Special Sales: specialsales@natgeo.com

For rights or permissions inquiries, please contact National Geographic Books Subsidiary Rights: bookrights@natgeo.com

Editorial, Design, and Production by Potomac Global Media, LLC

Designed by Jim Hiscott and Chris Mazzatenta

National Geographic Partners, LLC, and Potomac Global Media, LLC, would like to thank the following members of the project team: Kevin Mulroy, Eric Cline, Barbara Brownell Grogan, Kris Hanneman, Chris Mazzatenta, Karen Ang, and Tim Griffin. And from National Geographic Partners: Eva Absher, art director; Angela Modany, associate editor; Sarah J. Mock, senior photo editor; Debbie Gibbons, map director; Molly Reid, production editor; Anne LeongSon and Gus Tello, production assistants.

Hardcover ISBN: 978-1-4263-3002-5
Reinforced library binding ISBN: 978-1-4263-3003-2

Printed in Hong Kong
17/THK/1